"I always knew Kathy was funny. What I didn't know was that she really, truly understood me. At least that's how I felt after reading parts of this book. How did someone growing up in the South and in the country describe exactly how I felt growing up in a small town in the North. She proves once again that the human experience is universal. I can not wait to experience the entire book!"

—Carol Benefield,
Pawley's Island

"Kathy's homespun humor, coupled with her accuracy of a small town family, has caused me to unearth many a long lost memory ranging from my recalling the smell of gardenias on my grand momma's back porch to the eccentric behaviors we all accept as being Southern. In this day and time where tradition has either been forgotten or worse yet perceived as too rural, Kathy's twist on our culture has energized me to again embrace my southern ways and pass it along to the next generation."

—James F. (Jan) Harper,
Murrells Inlet

"A vibrant, beautifully written collection of Southern humor. Kathy weaves a vast, colorful tapestry of Southern life from a female perspective."

—Nancy Dunham,
North Litchfield

WHY, SHUT MY MOUTH!

4/09

Laugh a Lot and Always,

Kathleen Harper

"J"

by KATHLEEN HARPER

TATE PUBLISHING & *Enterprises*

Published by Tate Publishing & Enterprises, LLC
127 E. Trade Center Terrace | Mustang, Oklahoma 73064 USA
1.888.361.9473 | www.tatepublishing.com

Tate Publishing is committed to excellence in the publishing industry. The company reflects the philosophy established by the founders, based on Psalm 68:11,
"The Lord gave the word and great was the company of those who published it."

Book design copyright © 2008 by Tate Publishing, LLC. All rights reserved.
Cover design by Leah LeFlore
Interior design by Kellie Southerland

Published in the United States of America

ISBN: 978-1-60696-872-7
1. HUMOR / Topic / Relationships
2. COOKING / Regional & Ethnic / American / Southern States
08.11.11

To my friend Carol, that gave me
the inspiration to write.

To all of my family and friends that have
supported me throughout this process
and have given me many fond memories.

And to our Heavenly Father that gave me the
talent of writing, and hoping it will bring
joy and laughter to a lot of people's lives.

TABLE *of* CONTENTS

INTRODUCTION

outherners have a way with wit! *At least this gal does!* I'm an honest person and I will tell you here, up front and center, what I think and what other people have been thinking for years but just won't say it! *And why not?* It's the *dang* truth, so why shouldn't it be told? I guess people are afraid of hurting somebody's feelings or offending them, but my intent is neither of the above. I just wanted to bring to light a lot of the silly things that we think about and do, and this book isn't called *Why, Shut My Mouth!* for nothing.

I got my knack for humor honestly. My dad is a *"pistol"* himself. Growing up in a small town, there was never much to do, or you either didn't have enough money to do it with. I had to learn to use my imagination to come up with ways to play and entertain myself, and it has lasted into my adulthood. I have a lot to do now and a little more money to do it with, but imagination is a blessing, don't you think?

I love to laugh, tell a good joke, and tell things just like they are. I seldom *sugarcoat* anything. And if you don't want me to really explain something, don't ask me! 'Cause I will tell the truth in a skinny minute, will not leave out any details, and you can bet your *sweet britches* on that too!

I think laughter and poking fun at ourselves is a good way to relieve stress, hopefully will help us to live longer, and to definitely not take ourselves too seriously. No harm in it! Besides, it's my life and my lack of ulcers, so I'll deal with it.

I hope you will find some laughter while reading this book. All of it is true! I may have exaggerated a bit here and there, but it is all just the plain truth. I could have written about fictitious people and places, but what's the point? Real people and real situations are the funniest and capture people's curiosity a lot better, don't you think?

I did cheat a bit and change the names of many of my characters to keep people guessing. I tried to give them Southern names, since this is a humor book with a Southern *twang*. I also don't want to get a call from any of my lawyer friends, if you know what I mean.

I also have my "dang" family in here a lot, but mind you I love them to pieces, and you know you can always pick on your family. Besides, it's all in fun anyway, and we're notorious for making fun of each other, it keeps us going, and there's never a dull moment around here! We all live together in a small beach house on the coast of South Carolina, and both of my kids decided to come home again. *May the good LORD help me!* And I think He has, time and time again.

My pen name is Kathleen, but my given one is Kathy. My Grampy called me that when I was a *young 'un,* though no one can figure out why. I answered to it until the day he died. I sort of like it, since it does go well with my last name, and it gives me a cherished memory boost when I think about it.

I am not a novelist like my favorite Miss Dottie, who is also a Southern gal, and I can't write very good poems like my mother or my sister-in-law, but I can write about humor or at least participate in it a little bit every day. So I decided to channel my energies where my talents lie, and I hope you think so!

I want to thank my family for putting up with my tendencies to change occupations every week and for having the nerve to make one of my dreams become a reality. I also want to thank my good friend Carol, that put the *bug in my ear* to write, and I will be forever grateful. And to all you wonderful Southerners or Southern *wannabes* that decided to take a chance and read this book.

So let's go on a little journey together. I can't sing, but I can dance, and LORD knows I haven't quit my day job. Enjoy! As my grandmother Nanny also used to say, *"Why, shut my mouth!"* I dedicate this book to her and to all the people in my life that have given me many cherished memories and funny things to write about.

Sincerely,
Kathy

GROWING UP IN *the* SOUTHERN WAY

I decided to start this book off by telling you a little bit about my upbringing and to give you a little taste of what it's like to grow up in the *good ole South*. None of this is fiction, mind you, not too sassy, just the plain truth. I think this sets the mood for the rest of my stories and will help you see exactly where I'm coming from. 'Cause I'm as Southern as I can be and don't know much over the Mason Dixon line, wherever the heck that exactly is.

Southern folks are some of the nicest, most dear people in the entire world, and I am proud to be one of them. These folks are usually friendly, will speak and wave at everybody, tend to see the good in people, and love to talk (you know it takes us a while due to the accent). They can also be very cantankerous, just like my Grampy, who when he spoke, the grandkids would scatter! My family was mostly of English and Scotch/Irish descent. I don't remember any redheads, (unless it came from a box) but I do remember a lot of Irish tempers flying.

Southern dialect is so unique; ever try to get a Northerner or Westerner to try to speak Southern?

They totally mutilate it! *Or rather we have mutilated it, and they are just trying to fix it!* You have to be born and bred in the South to allow the words to slowly roll off your tongue just the right way: "Ya'll, Puh…lease, sit a spell, over yonder, how er ya'll doin, ain't no never mind, dang, mommer an 'em," are phrases that only a true Southerner can say with belief. Most of these phrases have been around for ages, and I think we might be one of the few that can make up things and get away with it.

I was born and raised in a little *"podunk"* town in the upper part of South Carolina; I call it the upstate 'cause it is straight up, but it is actually the Piedmont. (My definition of podunk is small, not much to do, have to drive a while to get to a big city.) I don't want to name it here, since those folks might not take too kindly to me calling it podunk. But I sure was, raised in Podunk, USA! *Raised means "reared," brought up, in case you're wondering*. Heck, South Carolina is so full of podunk towns, that mine would be hard to pinpoint. But, they are all great towns with good people, and I am proud that I am from one of them. I believe where you are raised and what you experience in your life builds your character, and I think my little podunk was a good one! I turned out all right, I guess! But you may beg to differ after reading this book.

I am a child of the late 50's who had young parents that were barely out of high school. Heck, my momma was still in high school. They managed to do okay. People in that generation got married young and didn't think a thing of it. Women usually stayed home and took care of the family and the household, while the men worked to support them. I think my daddy worked in the local cotton mill back then, where most of the town did earn a living. I often wondered if the mill closed down, where would everybody go or do? (Interesting, a lot of the original mill has closed down in the past five years, and the town is still *kicking!*)

Most of my family worked in the cotton mill at one time or another; they were just middle class folks, country some might say, hardly any of them were educated past high school. Some of them walked to work since they lived in the *mill village*. I don't remember many of them having cars, or if they did, they sat in the garage most of the time, if they had one. Two cars were unheard of back then. These cars were just plain cars too; no air conditioning (*whew*) and no fancy radio, just AM channels mostly, if they had one at all!

My great grandparents lived in one of those mill houses that had 3–4 rooms with high ceilings, a coal fireplace in the center of the house, a wood stove in the kitchen, and a woodshed in the back yard. *You didn't want to go there if you misbehaved!* It was a tight living space, not much privacy, but as a kid, it seemed much larger to me.

I remember a *big ole* (that's another Southern phrase) iron poster bed, homemade quilts that my great grandmother had made, gourds hanging in the breezeway (they used these to dip water or whatever), and a spit cup or two. (A spit cup is for tobacco, snuff, or for just plain spit!) My great grandmother liked to dip snuff, as did a few of my relatives, and this was just normal to me. Ever seen someone dip snuff? It ain't a pretty sight and a messy one at that!

I also remember the kitchen table always had a tablecloth on it, a round cake of butter, and a jar of blackstrap molasses. You could reach you hand in one of the top bins of the wood stove, grab a homemade biscuit, cut it in two, then put the molasses and butter on each half of the biscuit. But not before you took the butter and molasses and mixed it together in one big mess. (You actually sopped the molasses and butter mix with the biscuit, but nowadays it would be quite an uncouth way to eat.) I looked forward to that when I was a kid. Better than candy! And it didn't rot your teeth. "Don' eat too many sweets; your teeth will rot!" a lot of my old folks would tell me. None of my teeth ever rotted, so I guess I was okay.

Another thing I remember about that house is that my great grandmother had a foot long statue of Jesus on her dresser. I used to go by it and stare at it but never touched it until my mother inherited it a few years ago. I guess I had a lot of respect for it, or I was afraid of it, one. I never really knew where that statue came from, and I never asked. That statue made it seem like God was in the house, so you had to act respectful.

My father's mother, Grandma, lived in a clapboard house on the outskirts of town that had an outhouse in the backyard. (If you don't know what this is, you really are young!) For you young 'uns, it is a tiny clapboard building that was used as a toilet, because a toilet was a luxury way back then when the original house was built. Occasionally I would see my grandfather, Grampy, go in there, but it took me a while to figure out why would anyone want to sit on a wood box over a hole in the ground. And why was the Sears Catalog in there? I asked myself that when Grandma's chickens visited that hole too when somebody left the door open.

Lots of people had outhouses on the outskirts of town, but Grandma had a toilet and a bathroom, so we didn't have to go sit in one of those. I do remember the bathroom being ice cold in the winter since it was an addition after the original house was built, and there wasn't any heat in there. I remember *"holding it"* longer when I went to see Grandma. No one wants to put his or her delicate hiney on a cube of ice in the middle of the winter!

My mother's parents had running water but didn't have a hot water heater. Yes ma'am! They had to fill a very large pot of water and boil it on the stove and mix it with cold water that was in the tub. They had about four inches, if that much, to bathe in, and it better be good! No wonder people used to take a bath on Saturday night whether they needed it or not. *What a job!* When I was around 30 years old, my grandparents finally moved into another house that had a hot water heater so they could take a bath anytime they wanted to without having to boil their water supply. *And you know what?* My grandmother still wouldn't take a bath but once a week, because that is how it had always been. Tradition is hard to break, huh?

My grandmother, my Nanny as I called her, was a very proud Scotch/Irish lady that was as sweet as sugar, but she could *cuss like a sailor* when provoked. She was a very God-fearing lady and she would always tell us about the Bible and how we needed to be good. Nanny never went to church much, but I never saw a more loyal servant than she was. I remember one time she lifted her hand up to a beautiful rainbow that had just formed after a rainstorm and said "Do you see that rainbow? I don't see how anyone could not believe in God." She taught me a lot about life, loving, and living, and I'll never forget her. She went to be with the LORD about ten years ago, and I will miss her always.

My mother's father, Paul, was actually her stepfather, but there was no *"step"* in his fathering ability. He raised my mother from the time she was about five years old, and that was her daddy as far as she was concerned. He was my grandfather too! He took a *shine* to me when I was a baby and never let go until he went to be with the LORD too! He was a wonderful, sweet man that dodged my Nanny's tongue-lashing a lot, but would do anything for anybody at anytime. I was truly blessed to have him in my life.

Growing up Southern, I did spend a lot of time with my family, especially with all my grandparents, aunts, uncles, and cousins. My grandparents were my surrogate parents, and it was they who told me a lot of the stories that I hold with me today; let me make a mess in the kitchen when I insisted on baking a cake; ruined my grandmother's best towel because I wanted to wax the floor; would eat cupcakes until I threw up, because I wanted to and they didn't care. Grandparents are and should be the highlight of a kid's life. At least mine were, and I was lucky to be born to young parents, who also had young parents, so I was able to have them for a good part of my adult life. Most people aren't so lucky!

I lived in a small town for most of my young adult life. Conversations were long and interesting when I was with my friends or family, unlike today, where digital television, computers, and video games take up so much of a person's down time. People don't talk to each other like they used to, because there is always something playing that is more interesting. *Ain't that a shame?* I can imagine the stories that are missed and the memories that aren't created, because people focus more of their attention on technology. Well, enough of that! I did create a lot of memories by listening to my *old folks*. Heck, sometimes, if I didn't listen, they would give me a tour of that woodshed I was telling you about!

I didn't misbehave much. That's the thing about Southerners in my generation, they did believe in old-fashioned discipline. You grew up learning manners from the day you were born. Please, thank you, may I, called elders "Ma'am" and "Sir," asked to "be excused" (don't laugh here, we were not asking to go to the bathroom; maybe, maybe not!); didn't interrupt when the older folks were talking or you got the *"evil eye,"* and that usually meant you were going to get a *whipping* when you got home.

Now "whipping" didn't really mean that, but it probably felt like it. Today, it would be called *child abuse*, so I think it best not to go there. But, it did put the fear in us children when our parents talked about a whipping, so we tried our best to behave. Have you ever heard your mother or grandmother tell you to go and *"cut me a switch"*? I won't go there either. But if you ever see me, just ask, and I'll tell you all about it! If I ever did get a whipping or a switching, it was probably because I deserved it; sassing my parents, disobeying, etc. But after the punishment, I usually got a hug and some kind words from them. I never felt mistreated, only that I had learned a very valuable lesson and I had a sore behind to help me think about not ever doing it again.

Well, all in all, I think I had a pretty good childhood. Pretty good, meant plenty of food to eat, at least four changes of clothes a week (My momma made my clothes, and I had to wear Monday again on Friday if it didn't *stink* too bad!), had transportation to and from school on the bus, had a decent and very clean house, and always went to church on Sunday. I was born a Southern Baptist and stayed that way for thirty years (I don't judge anyone else's religion, so if you are saying *"that figures,"* just keep reading.).

You see, my growing up as a Baptist put me in the church on Sunday morning, Sunday night, and Wednesday night. I had to go whether I wanted to go or not. I was strongly encouraged or rather given the evil eye, so you didn't dare tell Momma or Daddy that you weren't going! I did go, and in the sanctuary I always sat on the back row with my friends. We passed notes, whispered, stared at the older boys in our group and thought about what we were going to do after church.

My younger brother used to sit on the front row of the church, shape his hand like a pistol, and shoot the preacher all during church. I never knew how the preacher could keep a straight face while that was going on. My parents knew I wasn't paying attention, and every Sunday in the car after church they would ask me what the preacher had talked about. I never had an answer, because I never knew. I guess you could say that church was really one of the highlights of my social life.

Getting back to growing up Southern Baptist, it

was all I knew for the majority of my young life. My first church was in the mill village where my great grandmother lived. The preacher was sort of the *"fire and brimstone"* type; he used to beat on the pulpit and scream at the congregation. (To a little person like me, it was screaming!) He would also get down on his knees and call out to God with his fists in the air and close his eyes real tight. Sometimes he would even take his glasses off and wipe his face with his handkerchief, he got so worked up.

I used to ask my momma why the preacher was mad at everybody, and she would always say, "Honey, he's not mad, he's just preaching"! Well, he seemed mad to me, so when I was little I was afraid of him, Preacher Johnston.

The preacher after that was Preacher Beecher, a short, roly-poly sort of man with a belly like Santa and hair to match. He was a nice little man and always winked at me. I wasn't afraid of him, but he did scream at the congregation just like Preacher Johnston did, but I guess I was a little older and had gotten used to it by now.

From hearing all this so much while I was growing up, I just thought all churches, preachers, and such were this way. But when I got married, I decided to try the Methodist church and realized that they didn't do all that screaming.

Oh well, that's enough about religion. I am a Christian, and I believe in the *Good Book*, as my Nanny used to say, and try to be a good example, and I try not to question any other folks' religious practices. What counts is whether the means is the way to an end, in other words, do whatever works and what feels right to you! That's the way I look at it.

Growing up in the South and living in the *"sticks,"* had some advantages that might look like disadvantages to non-Southerners! As a kid, I got to play in the woods, make forts, climb trees, eat wild strawberries, wade in the creeks, catch tadpoles, and just get plain dirty! That's when kids really knew how to play, instead of sitting in front of the television or those dang video games like they do today. We really did have to use our imaginations, because sometimes we didn't have anyone to play with.

There weren't any girls my age around my neighborhood growing up, so I had to play with boys most of the time. We would go barefoot, play kickball, ride bicycles, play cowboys and Indians or Army in the drainage ditches. We lived in a red clay area, and my clothes would be covered. I remember one time I went into a muddy "gulley" with some of the neighborhood boys and got covered with mud from head to toe. Momma made me strip down before she would let me in the house. Those days were fun though; my children really never got to experience any of that! We lived on the edge of the woods when they were growing up, but times have changed.

I could tell you a lot more about growing up in the South, but I'll elaborate more in the other chapters of this book. *Life is funny!* I think everyone is special and everyone has a story to tell. But for those of you that weren't raised in the South, where you were raised is probably very special too! The experiences that you have in your life make you who you are, so sit back, enjoy, and take my adventure with me! As my Nanny used to say, *"You better shut your mouth!"* when I was saying stuff that I shouldn't say, but stuff like this is good to share and helps to enlighten the soul.

At least I think so. And I hope you enjoy the rest of the sharing that I will be doing with you, and I might add a few sassy thoughts too!

A LITTLE GIRL, GRAND DADDY PAUL, *and* CRACKER JACKS

When I was born, my momma and daddy were very young and didn't have much money, so we all lived in a tiny clapboard house with my momma's parents: Nanny and Grand Daddy Paul. It was tight, because things were for everybody, but we managed. We lived there until I became a toddler, and I was the *apple* of my grandparents' eye. Especially for my Grand Daddy Paul!

Paul was my momma's stepfather, but he was all the father or grandfather that either one of us needed, at least on this side of the family. He had helped raise my momma and now he had a hand in raising me. Grand Daddy Paul was as much a part of me as if he were my flesh and blood. I was so lucky to have him in my life, and I think all of the grandchildren felt that way. My momma and her sister adored him and couldn't have asked for a better father; a kind and gentle soul that never really asked for anything in return. His children and his grandchildren were his blessing, and there wasn't anything that you asked of him, that he wouldn't do for you.

Grand Daddy Paul was a very soft-spoken man.

Hardly ever heard him raise his voice unless he was fussing with my Nanny, and they did that often. I guess their fussing must have fallen on deaf ears, since most of the family just ignored it or laughed at them. But the more someone else laughed, the poutier my Nanny got, and the sillier my Grand Daddy Paul got. I remember him saying, "Oh hush, Agnes!" and she would say, *"Why don't you shut yo' mouth!"* So you see where I get it from.

Grand Daddy Paul was also raised in the South, and he grew up during the Great Depression, which wasn't so great. He was raised mostly by his father, since his momma died when he was a little boy. I don't think he had much of a childhood, since he remembers being hungry and how he never had any money. I used to ask him about that a lot when I was little, and he used to tell me some good stories.

He was the thriftiest man I ever met. He always had a lot of money because he worked hard and saved every penny he made. Never had any fancy things and bought most things secondhand a lot of the time. He even brought things home from the garbage dump to try to fix them up. Their house had "garbage dump fixer-upper" chairs still in their living room, and they didn't look half bad. He wasn't ashamed of the fact that he had gotten them from the dump, but beamed at the fact that he had taken something that wasn't worth much, put his handyman touch to it, and made it into something nice.

My momma always said that Grand Daddy Paul probably had the first dollar that he ever made. And I would not doubt it one bit. He was thrifty, but he still managed to spend plenty of money on me when I was growing up: peanuts, crackers, ice cream cones, M & M's, cough drops, and always a box of Cracker Jacks.

Grand Daddy Paul was probably the principal person in my life to take me to the county fair. Every year my parents and I would pass by and see it being set up at the fairgrounds, and I would make sure that he knew it was in town. I delighted at the sight of the Ferris wheel, big tents, and straw being thrown all over the ground. Momma would give me some money, and Grand Daddy Paul would come and pick me up in his truck and away we would go.

He let me ride all of the rides that weren't too dangerous, and we would walk around for what seemed like hours. I always got a candy apple, which would almost pull my teeth out, cotton candy that would make my hands stick to everything and usually popcorn. We would go inside a big barn and see all of the farm animals, and I couldn't believe that cows and hogs were so big. They looked so small from the road.

I used to spend just about every Friday or Saturday night with Grand Daddy Paul and Nanny when I was a little girl, and every time I would go over there, there would be a box of Cracker Jacks sitting on the kitchen table. (That table was one of the 50's type with metal legs and a red top. I think it had red chairs to match.) I would open that box as soon as I saw it, dig in, and hunt for the prize. I always wanted the little book, but only got it about one third of the time. Then I would sit down in front of the black and white television with Grand Daddy Paul and watch all the old shows. My favorite was "Gomer Pyle," and it usually came on at ten o'clock and that was way past my bedtime.

During Gomer Pyle, Grand Daddy Paul would turn

on the porch light for Nanny, who always worked late, for her to come up the driveway by. She always rode with someone to work. Gas was cheap back then, but not if you didn't make a lot of money. She worked in the old Springs' cotton mill in the cloth room and inspected cotton cloth coming out of the loom. Grand Daddy Paul was a painter, and a good one at that, and he worked for the mill too.

Sometimes Grand Daddy Paul would take me to the laundromat, and we would wash clothes while we were waiting on Nanny to get off work. They didn't have a washing machine, heck they didn't have a hot water heater either; at least not until I was a mother for the second time, and it didn't seem to bother them either. Things like a hot water heater, an air-conditioner, and a washer and dryer were what they called *"conveniences,"* and if you didn't grow up with them, it didn't seem like a big deal not to have them.

I liked to go to the laundromat too, because he would buy me packs of peanuts or crackers out of the Lance machine while we were waiting for a nickel each. It was probably here that we had a lot of conversations about my life and such. Grand Daddy Paul liked to talk, and he especially liked to talk to me.

He always told me that I needed to get a good education, because he never got to go to school past the 1st grade, and never really learned to read well. He used to try to read the newspaper, but because he was uneducated it took him a long time. He did try to keep up with current events though and would never miss any of the evening news broadcasts. We always had to be home by the news hour, and if you couldn't find him at 6:00 pm, you knew where he'd be. Right in front of that television, and he didn't flip channels!

He wanted me to go to college and to go as long as I could. I remember one time he told me he wanted me to be a scientist, but I never really knew why. I did give him some of his wish and went through six years of college. Maybe it was his voice in the back of my head that helped me to reach for my goals. And maybe I keep on reaching because his voice is still there. I don't think anybody's ever too old to have goals.

Grand Daddy Paul was a great influence in my life, probably my whole life, and I wish I had told him more of how much I did appreciate him and what he had done for me. Some other memories of him are that he took me to my first steak house dinner on my 10th birthday, and both of us were all dressed up. He taught me how to drive a car on a column, cried at my wedding, and took up with my daughter when she was born, where he had left off with me. An incredible human being and one that can't be replaced.

I remember that he had a garden in his backyard that he used to grow just about anything that would grow in that red clay. One thing that I remember, and still have several pots of, were what he called *"hen and biddies."* It's a cactus-type plant that sprouts other little plants and grows over the side of a flowerpot. He used to have a lot of those. He also always had a big garden every year, and I can't remember a year that he didn't have one. One year Nanny sent him to the store to get twelve tomato plants, and he ended up coming back with twelve flats. So, bless his heart, he had brought home one hundred and forty-four tomato plants. Nanny gave him *"down the country"* for that.

If you don't know anything about tomato plants, they start very small and then grow very big, like six to eight feet tall. They produce a lot of tomatoes on one plant, so if you have several plants, you have enough to feed your entire neighborhood. Good thing the family liked tomatoes that year. *Ha!*

Grand Daddy Paul, I think, used the garden as his therapy. He liked to do things with his hands and he was good at it. This is probably why he chose the profession of painting. He taught me how to paint too, how to choose the right kind of paint, how to dip and hold your brush, how to brush with the grain of the wood or surface, and how to clean up your mess. I never was good at that last part; I just throw away the brush and buy a new one. Spoiled little southern belle, I am!

He also taught me how to drive a car, and this is well worth mentioning. You see, I learned to drive on not a stick shift, but where the shifting was done on the column of the steering wheel. I would love to see some of those prissy little girls of today trying to do that! It requires foot and hand coordination, and they probably wouldn't make it out of the driveway. *Shut my mouth!*

Grand Daddy Paul came day after day and we would go up and down my driveway until I could handle shifting and getting the rhythm of the clutch without cutting the car off. We probably had about two days to tackle this one. Bless his heart, that man had the patience of Job, and he never yelled at me once. In fact, my whole life, he never yelled at me for anything. Might have been very disgusted, but he didn't say much.

After we had tackled the driveway, we headed for the street in front of my house and then down to the stop sign. *Whew!* When I made it that far, I got to head out onto the highway. I bet we drove around about three weeks, doing this with him, until I finally felt like I had mastered this type of vehicle. *And guess what?* He gave me his old Chevy Impala, white with red interior and no radio, and no air conditioning, mind you! But I was so happy to get it, and it ran like a charm. I never minded that it didn't have some of the luxuries that we have to have now. And I know that he was beaming inside that he had given it to me.

Grand Daddy Paul and Nanny were very special to me my whole life, and I am so lucky for having had them, especially when I was growing up. I think it is a blessing to have grandparents, and I feel sorry for people that didn't get to have the experiences that I have had. Besides me, my children also were blessed to have them in their lives too! And I am thankful for that.

So if you have a dear grandparent, love them all you can and give them your undivided attention. Tell them how much you appreciate them, because at any minute your time could be cut short. Learn from them and cherish them…'cause child, they won't be here forever, and you will have missed out on one of life's many blessings.

Now get off your hiney and go give your Grandma and Grandpa a hug! Maybe even do something nice for them for a change, since they have probably invested a lot of time and love in you! Probably…I know they have. *Now get going!*

ME *and the* DANG CHRISTMAS LIGHTS!

Christmas is a special time of year in most places of the good ole USA, or whatever holiday you choose to celebrate. Holidays are so special, and the decorations are always beautiful. It's especially great in the South, but I'm a little partial you know!

My childhood Christmases were always filled with a fresh cut tree that was gotten from the woods behind our house; we never had a *"store bought"* one. *Never mind that my family was trespassing, but we won't go there.* Most of the time they were cedar, and they smelled so good. (That's the reason that my kids wanted a fresh one this year, they were tired of having a plastic headache from the artificial trees.) Mom would usually decorate it, and Dad would stay in the den and watch television, but we only had three channels back then. *But, what's the point of bringing this up?* You'll see in a few more paragraphs.

I've had some funny experiences with Christmas lights, or holiday lights, if you want to call them that. People in some places put them up and leave them up all year long. We always think they forget to take them down, but I bet they don't! You can find these lights up in the middle of the summer, along with plastic geese, artificial poinsettias, the works! My sister-in-law's neighbor likes to do that too, and it becomes March and they are still burning, and they should know better.

I've also had some horror stories with these dang lights. I have had some of the most aggravating things happen with them too. If they are last year's, and I am not the one to put them away, no one in my dang family wants to put them back in an organized manner without tangling them up. I think they just throw them in the storage bin. They don't replace the burnt out bulbs or throw the strings away that are all burnt out. "Just save it for Mom for next year so she can pull *all* of her hair out!" I know you can relate to this, and you know it's the truth!

Whoever said that we had to have lights anyway? Wouldn't just a few dangly bows give you the same thrill? No, you have to ruin someone else's Christmas every year by making them the keeper of the Christmas lights, and every year it just happens to be me. I think I'm getting a little carried away here, so I'll just finish the story.

It's now the holiday season in the Myrtle Beach area. I live here now; I traded Podunk for the South Carolina coast. Everywhere you see beautiful trees lit up with hundreds of lights, red velvet bows hung everywhere, and everything looks so spectacular. The only thing that you don't see is the poor soul that hung all those gosh darned lights and all the empty bottles of spiked *"whatever"* that they had to drink to do the job. I personally have my own stash of whatever, but I'm not telling anyone where it is! And I hope I remember where I put it; it's probably in one of those bins with the dang lights.

Did you know that you really can decorate a palm tree outside and make it look Christmas-sy? Never mind, the spikes and things on them that can cause you to puncture an artery, but they do handle a string of lights quite well. I like to take advantage of this, because it's the only time of year that I can decorate like I want and don't really ask for anybody else's opinion. I usually do it when no one is at home so they won't tell me how and when I should be doing it! But I don't usually listen to them about anything anyway, so they can just *shut their mouths!*

So yesterday I pulled out the house Christmas lights; those dang tiny little lights that everybody puts up, that look like bold glitter, icicles or a flickering frenzy when you plug them in. They sure are pretty, but a *pain in the butt* to put up!

First, I had to look under about ten large boxes, which are in the shop downstairs. (My husband cleans out the shop, and he stacks everything so high and heavy, you can't get to anything!) These lights looked pretty good for last year's batch, but only about half of them worked. I'd plug them in to see if they worked, put them up with my staple gun after almost stapling my fingers together a few times, and when I plugged them in, they wouldn't work. I gave the lights a good piece of my mind, which wasn't much by this time, and they still wouldn't come on. Pass me that spiked *"whatever"* and there better be plenty of it!

I strung the lights up, yanked the lights down for a good part of a Sunday afternoon. Finally I just yanked them all down, went to the dollar store, and bought all new ones. I also bought some little candles that when you twisted them, the lights came on. No more trying to find an outlet to plug the candles in! It was a good thought anyway, and just a thought it was.

I took all this stuff home, and went for round two. I put up all the lights again, and low and behold, they worked! Finally, I had beautiful icicle lights around my front porch. I had to use my ability as a trapeze artist to put them up though, since I live in a raised beach house, and the front porch is on the second story. I did have a dilapidated old ladder that was my father-in-laws and did try to use it. But I get a little impatient. I never secure the ladder like it should be, and what is the point of the top of the ladder if you can't step on it?

So I had to dance from piling to piling until I got those dang lights up! My porch is pretty high, so while I was dancing, I had to hold tight to the banister to keep from becoming a statistic or a 911 call for my neighbors. "What is she doing, and why is she doing it?" I can hear them saying, "Where is her husband?" Now that last question is something I almost never have the answer to.

Funny that should come up. *Why didn't I ask my husband?* He wasn't home at the time, and I'm stubborn, impatient, and won't wait for anybody. Isn't that just like a female, but we won't go there! When I want something done, it becomes a *do it now* moment, and there is a point in this story, and I will get to it later.

Getting to the candles, I took them out of the bag and put them together with AA batteries just like it said. I twisted the little suckers below the bulb so that the light bulb would come on. Well, every one of them did come on, and I put them proudly in the front windows of my house. Thought I did a good job too. Well, not exactly. I went outside to look at my creation, and the lights weren't bright enough. So, I took them all down, put my old candles back in the windows, and went around looking for light sockets. Oh well, I guess some things aren't meant to be. Sometimes the old is just good enough.

You think I would learn from that experience, that I am no expert in lighting! Well, I had to put some dang lights on the Christmas tree too and couldn't wait for help to arrive there either. My husband was at home by this time, but he was sitting on the couch doing what he does best: flipping channels on the television with his headphones on and had already gone to three different galaxies with the channels and was now headed to Planet Mars. He can't hear a blessed thing I say when he has those things on, so I quit trying! And it's probably a good thing that he doesn't, especially after I've gotten into my *whatever*!

Well, I go and get last year's lights that were for the tree; the tiny little white lights that say "if one goes out the rest stay on." *Yeah, right!* Maybe in your dreams! I bring all the lights out, go through the same thing that I went through outside, and found this time, that they all worked. *Glory be and hallelujah!* Well, I just went ahead and strung that live Fraser fur tree from the mountains of North Carolina with every bless-ed light that I had left. And never mind that I had to dance with that tree to string them too, and almost knocked it over a few times, and nearly *put my eye out* with a few of the needles. I was so proud, but aggravated that my channel-flipping husband hadn't even peeked around the corner to see what I was doing.

As soon as I got out the extension cord that I had just bought at the dollar store and plugged in those lights, only about half of them worked. *What the heck?* Well, not to be outwitted by Christmas lights, I just stung some others on top of these old burnt out ones and called it a day! My stash of *whatever* has seen to that, and I was far from caring at this point. Channel-flipping husband never knew a thing. And I didn't offer him any of my *whatever* either!

My story doesn't end here. My lights were really pretty for about three weeks, without even a bad flicker or a burnt out bulb, at least what you could see anyway. Then twas the day of the Christmas Eve party! Half the lights on my Christmas tree decided to die at once. I wanted to take that tree and throw her pretty burnt-out butt out the window, but I just strung some new lights over the burnt out ones. It's like trying to find a needle in a haystack with a magnifying glass to replace a bulb; I'd rather clean toilets in a metropolitan airport. *Dang Christmas lights!*

Oh, and to add insult to misery, those dang candles went out too! They lasted about a few days, and they went completely out. But, at least I had a warning with them. The Christmas lights just died an immediate death without the benefit of last rites.

My channel-flipping husband never knew the difference and said what a good job I had done on the decorations. He never knew I had to test drive all of them, go back to the dollar store several times to get new ones, string over the burnt out ones, and baby sit them everyday to make sure they were still burning.

Underneath his headphones and his trips to TV land, he had missed all of my fun!

Maybe next holiday season I should include him in the fun, and make his first challenge to find last year's lights and untangle them, 'cause I'm gonna put them away this year. *Ha!* That would give me a whole day to go shopping! I think I just might go *"on the wagon"* with the lights next year and partake of my stash of *whatever* instead, but make him go find his own.

P.S. After all of this ranting and raving, I must confess I went out after Christmas and bought more of the little glass *"demons"* for half price. And demons is putting it mildly! So see ya next year for part two!

IN DEFENSE *of* MY
CHANNEL-FLIPPING HUSBAND

My husband is one of the kindest, most loveable men that you would ever want to meet. (At least that's what they tell me. *Shut my mouth!*) He was raised in the good ole South, just like me, by a very Southern family. His roots are in Marlboro County and Clio, South Carolina. Blink once, and you've missed Clio if you go down Hwy 9. Blink twice and you've gone completely through Marlboro County.

Clio, bless her soul, did raise my husband to be a fine Southern gentleman, just like his Daddy, and his Daddy before him. Gentlemen open doors for ladies, pull the chair out when they come to a table, help them with their sweater or coat, and basically look after them while they are in their company. Nice manners and politeness are part of this gentle rearing and qualities that most gentlemen possess. Well ... that is until after the honeymoon!

I've been married for nearly twenty-one years to this wonderful man. He is great but has his faults and idiosyncrasies like all men. And believe me, *all* men have some of the very same habits. I've had a lot of men come, go, and stay in my life, such as my daddy,

Grampy, Granddaddy Paul, my uncles, my brother, my cousins, coworkers, boyfriends, etc. I've seen all ages, shapes, sizes, personalities, career paths, education levels, religions, you name it! And I bet I could pick out five things or *quirks* that they all have in common.

Now let me see, which five do I want to write about, since they have so many...

1—Men love remote controls!

Would you like to argue with me about that? Pass by any electronic or television/audio equipment store and guess what sex is carrying and flipping the remote? *Certainly not the women!* They are probably four aisles down from their male companion looking in the shoe department.

At my house, my husband will go into a panic if he can't find the remote control. I have watched him look for one for hours! He will turn my den upside down, flipping the couch cushions up and over, looking under the furniture, and then he'll turn to me and swear that I've put it somewhere. *Me?* Why, my hands never touch it when he's in the house, and besides, I only watch one channel. He's so delirious by this time that he doesn't realize that he could just push one button on the TV to turn it on, and one with an arrow to move the channels.

I have lived with this type of delirious behavior for so long that when he loses things and blames it on me, I just sit there and watch the show each time. *Dang television and dang remote control!* I bet my husband has gained thirty pounds since the invention of these, because he won't expend any calories to walk across the floor to turn on the television. Ain't that a shame but downright hysterical too!

2—Men can't find a dad-blasted thing!

Would you care to argue with me now? This may not be true for the single man that has a house or apartment or trailer of their own, but it is darn true of the married one.

Since I have married this supposedly smart, Southern gentleman, when it comes to finding something, his brains go completely out the door. Then he accuses me of hiding it from him. Everything he misplaces or loses, I hear, "Kat, where did you put so and so?"

Kat never put it anywhere. Sometimes it is right under his nose, or under something, or in the wrong drawer, or in his car, or in his coat pocket or under his seat. I could go on and on. Shall I recall that he has had to have his checkbook mailed to him three times from a hotel because he left it on the back of the television? Probably confused it with the remote. Oh well, he's still looking, and I'm still watching him flip.

This shouldn't be mentioned, but he has a false tooth that he takes out at night. He loses it at least weekly, but I may be exaggerating a little bit here. I have seen him run through the house frantic, but run is a harsh word and totally untrue, to find that tooth that I hid from him. *You know that is my life's ambition!*

Oh well, that tooth has literally *"walked"* all over this house. One time, he left it on the table and the dog decided to have a taste. That tooth was a little *whop sided* after that, to say the least. And what was funny was watching my husband talk with it in his mouth. *I really should be shot for saying that!*

3—Men can't tell time.
Not if they won't wear a watch!

You are realizing I might be telling the truth by now. My husband has a watch but won't wear it. It's an anniversary watch, and he's afraid he will scratch it. So I guess I'll bury him in it; no risk of scratching it there! *(Shut my mouth!)*

No, seriously, if he tells me he will be back in an hour or two, usually multiply by three, and you'll get it right. The same if he tells you he will be home from work in *"a little while."* You can almost time him by that equation.

My husband and his predecessors have had no sense of time when it comes to watching sports on television. They can stay in one spot, on the same network, all day from dusk till dawn and never move except to take the occasional *"pit stop"* and refrigerator run.

"Why do ya'll do that?" I ask.

My answer is, "You're not a man, so you wouldn't understand."

Thank God! But just let you go out for an afternoon of shopping and you tell him you will be back in a little while. Your cell phone might go off a few times while you're shopping, just to check on you. When you get home, all you hear is "where have you been? Took you long enough, do I have any money left, we're out of Diet Cokes, and, oh yeah, what's for supper?" Another fault, they don't listen either, unless it's a commercial or a game score is being called out!

4—Men never get in a hurry to take out the trash or any chore for that matter and that's an understatement!

How many times have I asked him gently, without raising my voice, to puh—lease take out the trash? Take this as an example: I have several large bags that are so overflowing that a twist tie won't close them, they smell, and if they tip over, I'm going to have a mess. And I will not be happy!

Every so gently, I walk toward him with a loving, gentle voice and say please. (I'm getting dramatic just to make a point here.) He looks at me with those masculine facial features and piercing eyes and says, "I'll get it later!" My adrenaline explodes, my heart starts pounding, my face gets red, and my fists start to ball up! I am suddenly going to lunge at this man with all my might and proceed to kill him if he doesn't take out my trash. He probably knows I mean business by this time by my bulging eyes and crazed look on my face. The response I get from him by this time is, "What? You are the most impatient woman that I know!" He should retract that statement. The other women I know would have killed him by now.

5—Men never wipe the crumbs off the counter or any place else for that matter!

If you find a man that does, send me his name and phone number, and I will send him a letter of congratulations. And I will also faint at the sight of him, because he will be a figment of my imagination.

My husband will clean up the dishes, or rather load them in the dishwasher, put almost everything up, leave the kitchen, and he is done. Crumbs are still rampant and will stay there until I come along and wipe them off or the neighborhood ants want to come in for a snack.

He will literally get up every morning with the same crumbs on his mat where he eats his breakfast, and there they will stay. I sometimes wonder, doesn't it get scratchy putting your elbows on the same crumbs everyday? Jelly might be there too, but it doesn't seem to bother him. There are always coffee grounds around the coffee pot, and they greet me every morning too! And the funny thing is that he sometimes will wear these little critters to work, if I don't run behind him and stop him before he leaves the house. *Ew!*

Little things like crumbs do bother me, but to the men I have observed in my life, they seem invisible to them. I have watched several of them rake them in the floor to get them out of the way, and I have wanted to scream. I could tell you what they had for breakfast, lunch, and dinner by the evidence that is left behind. Maybe that is how my mother knew things about us when we were growing up, and we didn't have a clue!

My husband, and men in general, are funny creatures. No, I guess they are just different from us, and things that make us women crazy don't matter so much to them. But we love them, they're our family and friends, and I really don't think we would change them much if we could. Just train them to take out the trash on command, and that would be a start!

Bless their little channel-flipping hearts!

"PEARLS" IN NEW YORK

A few years ago I took a trip to New York with my sister-in-law, Sarah Lane, and our "Pearl" friends. You see, this was my very first trip to the Big Apple, and this group of ladies gave me a very interesting ride. Or rather, I gave them one! With a bunch of true Southern belles in New York City, your ride might be very entertaining and give you enough stories to talk about for a long time to come. And we're still talking about it!

The "Pearls" are a group of ladies that are all Southern, either by birth or by location. They all have a Southern accent (maybe), understand the Southern dialect, and have Southern manners. They all like to wear pink, put on cultured pearls and earrings elegantly, and love to play a mean game of Bunko. Some like to swear under their breath, can say *"kiss my assets"* in the kindest way, talk about their weight problems, and will eat the nearest café out of cheesecake if they take a notion to! They all have different personalities, different ways of expressing humor, different idiosyncrasies, but they all share a love of laughter and take delight in being called "Southern." So let me tell you this funny story!

This adventure started in the airport of Myrtle

Beach, South Carolina. We had all met to board our plane to go to the Big Apple on a cool night two weeks before Christmas. There were seven of us "Pearls," and we were all excited and giddy to be able to go to the city for shopping, eating, and such. "Such" is a big word when you describe these women. We had padded our pocketbooks and loaded down our suitcases for a four day excursion that would give us a lot of laughter.

Let me first introduce the "Pearls" to you. I am not going to use their real names, 'cause I don't want them to come knocking at my door pointing fingers and telling me that it's all lies. Remember what I told you at the beginning of this book: I only write the truth, because real life is the funniest. Besides, some of their husbands are *well-to-do* attorneys or one of their Pappy's is an attorney, so I don't want them to come a' knocking.

Pearl #1—Sarah Lane

She is my sister-in-law, and what a true Southerner she is! She is prim, proper, doesn't swear in mixed company, and has a little spark of Miss Scarlett about her; Scarlett's temper that is! Especially when it comes to South Carolina Gamecock football…but we won't go there. *Yes we will!* I am a Clemson University graduate, and Clemson did beat Carolina this year, but that's all I'm going to say. And that is all the information she needs.

She's the shortest one of the bunch, but she can pack a punch with her knowledge of politics and the school system. (I don't know a dang thing about either one, and my husband is a principal.) She is a very sweet gal, and I am proud to call her my family, even though she is a Gamecock fan! I'll be kind to her, though, because her husband is an attorney, soon to be a district judge, and I want to stay on their good side. I may be Southern, but I ain't crazy!

Pearl #2—Georgia

This lady is the most outspoken one of the group, but she is one of the most loveable women I have ever met. She comes from a fine North Carolina family, which have dabbled in politics themselves. Georgia could lead or rather coerce the masses to do whatever she wanted them to. She also was our *"cruise director"* for this trip, so her leadership was a much-needed talent for us, especially those that were rookies like me. She also has a laugh that you can hear for miles, so the cabbies' honks didn't have anything on her. She and her family helped to save us when we moved to the coast, and we'll be forever grateful.

Pearl #3—Barbara

This gal is one of the funniest women I have ever met. She has a genuine cackle that you can hear for miles, just like Georgia, so they were a good pair and also roommates on the trip. Barbara likes to sleep in a freezer or an igloo as she calls it. Bless her heart; she has a lot more hot flashes than the rest of us. At night she built a fort around her with pillows, plugged up her fan, and proceeded to try not to turn her room-mates into popsicles. She also traditionally goes to bed at 5 o'clock pm, (lies, all lies) and during our trip she actually stayed up till one am without missing a beat. Never a dull moment when this gal is around!

Pearl #4—Priscilla Sue

Heck, I don't know if her middle name is Sue, but I like it! She is one of the most genuinely sweet people that you would ever like to meet. She is also a genuine coastal girl and grew up in the area of Murrells Inlet and has stayed there for most of her life.

Priscilla Sue also has a beautiful house on the inlet, and I can't for the life of me understand why she doesn't live there. The sunsets are breathtaking! Well, this was her first trip to the Big Apple, and she handled it pretty well, considering she went with this group of Southern belles.

Pearl #5—Margaret

I'm not sure if she was truly a Southerner, but she blended well with all of us. A nice gal, with a nice personality, and rolled with all the punches that we had to dish out. She must have been pretty special, because she came with Priscilla Sue, and they had been friends for years. Being friends with a "Pearl" says a lot!

Pearl #6—Marilyn

This woman has Southerner written all over her face. She has the sweetness and the manners of a true Southern lady. Impeccably dressed, very prim and proper, I bet she gave the New Yorkers a run for their money, or rather made their heads turn with every Southern breath. Marilyn and I were roommates, and I have never seen anyone's suitcase so neat, or who could find a place to put all of the ten pocketbooks that she bought. (In case you were wondering, pocketbook is a Southern word for purse, handbag, etc.)

Last, but not least,
Pearl #7—myself, Kathleen

Well, I am the last lady to be noted. I didn't know this crew that well when I agreed to go on this trip. I consider myself a true Southerner, in speech and in spirit. I wouldn't consider myself quiet though; I'm in the middle between Georgia and Barbara. I'm loud, opinionated, mischievous, humorous, and a pain in the butt when I want to be. But, I am the youngest Pearl, at least on this trip, so there! *And vanity is ever' thang!*

Well, let's get back to the story, since you've been properly introduced. We made it in one piece to the LaGuardia airport after a very short flight. The only complaint we had was that we had to pay for a decent snack on the airplane. *What's up with that?* Luckily one of our Pearls had a stash of food and was able to share with the rest of us. Ain't nothing like Chex Mix, M & Ms, and cheese crackers when you're starving half to death.

After retrieving our luggage after landing, and putting on fresh lipstick (gotta have those puckers painted), we headed to the van to take us to the hotel in exciting Manhattan. But not before our dear Margaret got her foot caught in the door of the van and almost *busted her assets*. We all then crammed in to the vehicle with our pocketbooks and headed out.

On arrival at the hotel, we came to a room full of elevators. *Which one?* I asked myself. I'd never seen so many in one area. I just joined in follow the leader and went with the rest of the crew into one and headed for the 8th floor. Never heard of a front desk on the 8th floor before, but this is New York. At the desk, Georgia checked us in, but not before striking up a conversation with the front desk clerk and learning his life's history. *"Who's your Daddy?"* is a common phrase around our house. And I bet Georgia knew that after our check in. Then she and Barbara disappeared. Those two "Pearls" just left us in the lobby!

The rest of us looked around for an elevator and got on, pushed #23, and away we went. There was glass inside and everything, not much breathing room though, so we held our breath. Coats and pocketbooks take up a lot of room! Funny smells do too when you want to get away from it. I do remember some young 'un saying *"Who farted?"* and it was all we could do to get off the elevator without choking with laughter. That's what Southern women do: they laugh a lot and out loud and will get tickled with just about anything!

On the 23rd floor, no Georgia and Barbara! We walked up and down the halls like a bunch of hillbillies, yelling for them, since we didn't know the room number. Finally we found them, actually heard them *"hee-heeing"* behind the door. I told you about those mile range chuckles. Well, when the rest of us five walked in the door, those two "Pearls" had their suitcases unpacked, had changed clothes, and were sitting on the bed and said "Where ya'll been so long?" and the reply was *"Kiss my assets!"*

The rest of us looked around, and the only place that we had to go was into the adjoining room. Sarah Lane had bargained with the rest of us to put up with Georgia and Barbara, so she bunked with them. But let me rephrase that! She didn't put up with them, she just found it in her best financial interest to be a little colder and have a little noisier area to sleep in during our trip. That's putting it lightly. So the other four of us went behind door #2, and those other girls stayed in the *"igloo."*

After we got settled and caught our breath, everyone decided that they were hungry. It was about 1:00 am and way past Barbara's bedtime. Well, we all got our coats back on and headed for the door. This time all-together! (Except for Marilyn that had already had enough and decided to *"put er down"* early.) The rest of us went down to the bottom floor and out into the streets of Times Square. *Honk, Honk, Honk, flash, flash, flash.* We "Pearls" had finally arrived. We were ready for Manhattan, but was Manhattan ready for us?

Out into the night we went. Back home everyone would have been in bed by now, especially Barbara! Can't for the life of me understand why these New Yorkers like to stay up so late? Down to Foxy's Deli we went, all six of us. The cheesecake in the window looked out of this world, and all of us were looking forward to a piece. Southerners never eat this late, but we were in New York, so who cares?

We all trampled into the café and settled into three booths in the back. People all around us were eating big plates of pasta and burgers. All of them had a bowl with green things in it, and we finally decided that they were pickles. We were all looking around, probably staring (not a nice trait for a Southerner), and making a little bit of noise, no, a lot of it! We are not a quiet bunch, so this would have been hard for us. We tried to see what the other patrons were eating; so then we decided to order. Most of us ordered the delectable cheesecake, but Barbara, bless her heart, ordered onion rings! But check this out, she pulled the onions out, and ate the batter with ketchup! (Looked a little backwards to me, no, very backwards, *but shut my mouth!*)

After our snack and patron entertainment, we decided to take our Southern butts to bed! Enough adventure for one day! Or so I thought. I happened to look out our window into the next building to see a gentleman lying in the window exercising his hands, and so late at night. At least that is what it looked like! Silly me! Barbara saw him too and let out a big cackle and everybody else came running to see what was going on. We've never heard the end of that one.

After a fairly good night's sleep, the second day of our trip started bright and early. A quick breakfast and not enough coffee put us back out into the streets of Manhattan. We walked fast, faster, and faster to get through those traffic lights. He, who hesitates, gets run over by a taxi, and I'm not kidding either. Dang near had to jump on the hood of one to get him to stop. Glad I wore my walking shoes!

I don't quite recall the order of all of our adventure's events, so I'll just hit the high and most humorous parts of the story. But I did manage to stop the "Pearl" pack for just a minute or two to peek at one of those street vendor carts with all the stuff on it: hats, scarves, pocketbooks, watches, New York souvenirs, you name it. A couple of minutes turned in to about twenty, but I did manage to buy me a genuine imitation angora hot pink hat and a hot pink muffler to match. I was now *"styling and profiling"* and felt very New York! The other "Pearls" bought stuff too. You know a bunch of women can't resist a bargain, especially at $5.99 a pop!

After our shopping spree, we were on the loose and headed for Rockefeller Center and *The Today Show*. I was mesmerized by all the crowds, cameras, and celebrities. Things look a lot different on television. I was trying to get as close to the temporary fencing as I could without putting someone's eye out or stepping on someone's toes. Oh…I forgot to tell you that Sarah Lane had gotten pink pearls and earrings to match for everyone, and we wore them all the way there. (They looked nice with my new hat!) Also with handmade signs that said "Pearls" on them. We did get a lot of attention, chuckles, stares, evil eyes, but we took it all in fun!

After getting a *"stones throw"* from Al, Ann, but not Katie, we proceeded to our next activity: the stores of Fifth Avenue. Pretty window scenes everywhere! The stores were all decorated for Christmas and people were everywhere. I was so taken by the sight that I went the wrong way in one of the window viewing lines and almost knocked over several people, but not without the proper *"excuse me."* Southern girls are always polite, even while they are knocking the *mess* out of someone, but not intentionally, ya'll.

One of the first stores we went into we were reminded that there was no picture taking in there. You know, Southerners like to take pictures of everything, so this was a little disappointing. Then Georgia said later that we wouldn't be able to copy their jewelry design either, but we won't go there. *(Shut my mouth!)*

Our next stop was at some soda shop that has a famous name, which sounds like *serenity,* and has the best frozen hot chocolate! Think it was in some movie or something. Oh well, the frozen stuff was great.

But how in the heck can you call something hot that is frozen? We had a nice time there, but all the girls wanted to do is take pictures, laugh, and entertain the masses. We did get out of there in one piece, and weren't asked to leave, so I guess we did all right.

By this time our feet were killing us, and we didn't stop for breaks. My feet hurt so badly in one store that I sat down on one of the displays. *There was a chair in it, and never mind that I had to rearrange a couple of things.* I have no pride when my feet hurt that bad. Ended up buying a chocolate bar, so if they said anything about me sitting in their display, at least I had contributed to their income. Southern belles have no shame when their feet hurt! If I could have found someone to massage them right then and there, I would have paid 'em! *Then the display would have had to have some major rearranging!*

Our next stop was to go to the subway station and catch the train to the south end of Manhattan. (I kept seeing subway signs, but in my neck of the woods, it's a sandwich shop, so I thought it was an eating-place!) *Silly me!* You can't take this Southern gal anywhere. You can, but there are no guarantees as to her interpretation.

The subway ride was fun and interesting; you could get hung in the door real easily if you don't move fast enough. But we didn't, and got on without any problem. We also talked to everyone on the subway, and in the movies, you just *don't* do that in New York. And you know everything you see in the movies is real. People didn't seem to mind though, so it makes you wonder. I think most people are nice if you give them a chance. I told you Southern people tend to see the good in others! You also can't outtalk us; we win the prize there!

When we came to our stop, it was pouring down rain, but it didn't slow us down one bit. We were going to head to Chinatown once we exited the subway, but not before we were approached by three teens wanting to hustle us to buy their subway tickets. Contributing to their college fund we said, so we purchased the tickets and then hurried off. Never had that happen before, but it was New York.

Putting up our umbrellas, we went down to try to see the Statue of Liberty, but the fog was too thick. Not thick enough for the street hustlers with their watches, pocketbooks, and other things. And of course, Southern, naive women *have* to look at everything and want to get the most for their dollar, and must be polite in every circumstance. Well...we were too polite and long in doing so. Before we knew it, our hustler friends were run down the street by our local law enforcement without batting an eye. No harm done! But our bargains ran with them. *Shoot!*

The group then headed to Chinatown, which ended up being an all-afternoon adventure. Umbrellas cocked, we braved the cold and the rain to try to find the best bargains that we could. After the purchase of around twenty pocketbooks between all of us, speaking to every Asian American in Chinatown, we were starved. No country diner in this neck of the woods, so we decided to try some local cuisine: a noodle house. We approached a café-looking building that had dead fowl in the window. Literally, a dead duck and chicken with the head still on it. *As the stomach churns*, I said to myself.

Well, our tour guide Georgia went up to an Asian American man in the doorway, obviously the owner, and said that we had seven for lunch. This man then looked back at her with wild eyes and said "Seven!" in the most peculiar way. He then went over to the largest table with a couple that was finishing their meal obviously, and told them that they had to go because he had other customers waiting. I had never seen anybody do that before, but I had then. The couple looked quite perturbed, got up out of their seats, and left. We were then motioned by the man to come and have a seat.

Not really understanding what had taken place, I followed the rest of the "Pearls" to sit down. I looked around, which looked like such a cramped little place, and we had the biggest table in the café, but there were only about five tables! By the looks of the dead birds in the window, I was hesitant to order anything. The place smelled very odd, and I wasn't sure that noodles were what I wanted to eat, or any other strange things for that matter. And definitely not any dead fowl!

After much contemplation, I did order a bowl of noodles for $3.50 and decided that that was a bargain in Manhattan. Also, one of the strangest ways of getting something to eat that I had ever experienced. I didn't get sick after about thirty minutes, so I decided that the food must be okay. But that smell... *Ugh!* And I know that isn't a polite thing to say, but it's the dang truth.

After our lunch, the "Pearls" picked back up, went back out in the rain to the subway station, and headed for Times Square. This time we were headed to the discount theater ticket booth. *Yee ha!* You know Southern belles love a bargain!

Well, we got in line and stood for thirty minutes or so with the rest of the *"save a buck"* tourists in Manhattan. We did get tickets, but to *Little Women,* which turned out to be good, but our seats were in the nosebleed section. You do get what you pay for! Most of us were cold, tired, and downright ornery since we had walked from dawn till dusk and were ready for bed. Georgia and I even sat on the top steps at the side of the theater and watched most of the play. We had had enough culture for one day!

The third day we got up and headed out again. When we got to the ground floor of the hotel, a television show was being filmed and we saw the CSI guys go upstairs. How exciting, but since we had already seen so much, we just glanced and kept going. I think they even said that we could come up and watch, but we said "How nice!" and kept walking. We weren't impolite, but our feet kept moving! No celebrity chasing that day.

This time we headed for the St. Patrick's Cathedral. What a gorgeous and serene house of worship! We were all in awe as we walked up and down the aisles of this massive architectural structure. There were lit prayer candles at multiple altars throughout and each of us lit one and said a prayer. Growing up Southern Baptist and fairly modest, I had never seen such a fine place. This was supposed to be a quiet place where people come to pray, ask for forgiveness, and remember a loved one. We did too, but our group is rather loud, and with several loud chucklers in the pack, you could still hear us for several blocks. The people were nice and didn't run us out of there, but I've never heard of God asking anyone to leave His house. *We would have been the first!*

After our visit, we exited through the massive doorway, down the steps and spilled out into the streets, literally. I almost fell on the huge stone steps, tripped on my coat, and almost soared into another group of tourists. Not "Pearls," but tourists nonetheless; other bargain hunters.

With a group discussion, we decided to head toward the Rockefeller Center Christmas tree. It wasn't dark yet, heck it was still morning, so we couldn't really experience it until it got dark, but we headed in that direction anyway. Once at the base of the tree, and I was in awe just to be there, we took a lot of pictures. You know, the touristy thing! We even found some fellow Southerners to take our picture. *Fancy that!* Their clue must have been the cackling and the big pocketbooks. We stayed for a few minutes and headed down the street to a toy store.

I was expecting the same scene as I had seen in that movie with the little boy that puts his hands on his cheeks and yells, *"Ah...!"* You know, he gets left by his parents. We were told by one of the toy soldiers at the door that it had been remodeled. It was still an experience though, looking at all of the rooms and rooms of toys. I did get to dance on the floor size piano, which was also in some movie, but I forgot the name of it too.

I sure was mesmerized by everything that I had experienced so far. I had heard about New York City my whole life, and I was finally here. *Southern Mill Hill Gal* had arrived in the Big Apple! And I thought I might like to stay for a little while longer. There was lots to see and lots to do; definitely a change from Podunk!

I don't remember much after this, but I do remember that we decided to split into groups and not do everything as a whole. Me, Margaret and Pricilla Sue decided to take a taxi ride and go down to *Ground Zero*. My feet hurt so bad that I didn't care where the cabbie took us, so he rode us around for thirty minutes before arriving in Lower Manhattan.

After a long and speechless ride, the cabbie pulled us up to the site, and I was blown away. I could not imagine how anything as terrible as 911 could have happened in this place. I was so torn that I could not speak. Television had shown me the horror, but I was now standing on the burial ground. *All I could think of was God Bless the people who died here, and God Bless America.* I have never felt such a sense of sadness like that in a long time. And to this day, when I think about it, it still blows me away.

After a few minutes of taking this all in, we crawled back into the cab and drove back to Rockefeller Center. The cabbie didn't take us all the way there, but he let us out a few blocks away. I really didn't question this, seemed a little strange, I don't think he *spoke Southern*, so I just got out with Priscilla Sue and Margaret and proceeded down the sidewalk to the Christmas tree. Little did I know that some of our friends were having an adventure with the cabbies too!

Georgia and Barbara had gone together to try to get inside the Plaza Hotel to wait for the High Tea and they took a taxi. Before the cab took off, Georgia shut her coat in the door without knowing it, and it drug on the street all the way to the hotel. Barbara tried to be sophisticated and told the driver, "The Plaza, please," in a deep, non-Southern voice. Georgia tried to keep from cracking up and tried to keep a straight face. I'm sure the cabbie thought they were two rich broads or two *"dip sticks."* And I'll make a Southern bet on what he really thought.

After these two girls were dropped off at their destination, they tried to sachet up to the lobby of the hotel when they were politely asked to *stop!*

"But we were just going to the tea and into the lobby!" they said.

The Bellman gave them a strange look and said, "I'm sorry, but the tea is full, and you can only see the lobby at certain times." But it was eleven o'clock in the morning and it wasn't until three in the afternoon. *Then how dang early did you have to get there? The night before?*

Shocked and in disbelief the girls turned around and headed back out onto the sidewalk.

"Well, what do we do *nah…oh*?" I could imagine both of them saying. Its funny how you know people so well that you can put words in their mouths, or ah…heck, just make up something!.

Well, as disappointed as they were, they tried to get another taxi to take them to Rockefeller Center, as I had told them to meet us there by the *big tree*. As soon as they hailed a cab, just barely got the words out of their mouths, the cabbie didn't even bring the car to a complete stop. He just looked at them with wild eyes and sped off. By dusk, the Center was mobbed with people everywhere, and you probably couldn't come within a few blocks of it in a cab. I guess everyone is looking at that tree. This is my point to the previous cab ride with me, Priscilla Sue and Margaret.

Georgia and Barbara, by this time, decided that they would take a bus. *Ha!* Easier said than done. First, they had to dig in their pocketbooks for some *correct change only* for the bus fare! While digging, they lost some of their change on the sidewalk, and even had someone come up to them and ask if they had any to spare. *Spare change?* You never ask a Southern lady for her last dime or you might get a piece of her mind that you don't want to hear. Well, Georgia almost let this person have it in a toned down, only one block audible voice, and proceeded to dig in her pocketbook. Luckily, between both her and Barbara, they both came up with enough correct change to get on the bus.

The bus ride wasn't much better either! They tried to use their cell phones to call the rest of the "Pearls," but they were laughing so hard, and the bus was so loud, how in the heck did they expect for us to hear them. But at least they were on their way to Rockefeller Center and hopefully the bus wouldn't dump them out before they got there.

All during this time, me, Priscilla Sue and Margaret did get to the Center in one piece, by cab nonetheless, and walked the rest of the way. Sarah Lane and Marilyn, who I forgot to mention, were shopping and getting medication to ease an ailment. I don't remember any drama about their excursion; all I recall is that Marilyn bought a lot of clothes and closed the warehouse down while Sarah Lane sat in a chair and welcomed the rest to her tired feet. *And I guess she couldn't find anybody to massage them either!*

After most of us arrived at Rockefeller, we moseyed our way to a side street to a quaint café. We were hungry, tired, or sick and tired of walking, and just wanted to sit down and relax for a while. We were communicating with Georgia and Barbara by phone, and I kept telling them to turn right at the tree. Not good directions in a place as big as Manhattan, but it always worked well at home. Well, they kept walking and talking, walking and talking, and finally made their way to the café. I got some evil eyes when they walked in, but that was okay. *By this time I was too tired to care!*

After filling up with paninis, salads, pizza, cannolis, and I don't know what all, we decided to walk back to our hotel. We had had enough taxis, cabbies, buses, pretend tour guides, wrong directions, rain, and café food to last us for a while. We loved Manhattan, but we were ready to call it a day! And we did!

After a restless night's sleep that ended at 4:30am, we got up to get ready to catch our plane back to the good ole South. We were still tired, a little red or dry eyed being that it was winter, but we managed to get all of us in a cab to go back to the airport. Try to get dressed and packed with only two bathrooms for seven Southern belles. *Just ain't practical!* Not even enough room for all of our hair and bath stuff, and a gal has got to have all of that; it's a necessity of life! But we managed.

During the cab ride to the airport we all but froze to death since the windows in one of the cabs wouldn't roll up all the way, and we were stuck with the twenty degree breeze all the way to the airport. *What a wake up call!* Oh well, we were going home, so we might as well have one more bout of torture before we left.

For me the city was great, shopping and eating were fantastic, and it was an adventurous place to visit. But visit it will stay! My heart and soul belongs in the South, next to the ocean, and yes I do like the *"rotten smell"* of the marsh. I like quiet sunsets, not flashing lights all the time. I like wind on my face, but not from a speeding cab. I like to hear the waterfowl cries, not loud music unless I'm doing housework, and definitely don't like to see them hanging in any noodle house window. *Oh well, I am just a Southerner at heart!*

But...I'd go back to Manhattan in a skinny New York minute! With "Pearls" or no "Pearls"! And I've made it back several times since then. And I'm now contemplating my next trip...when my husband ain't looking! And trying to find another piece of luggage to take with me, to hide all of my *"findings."*

Nah...I'll just buy it there.

HUMOR IN *the* OFFICE

I work in one of the local hospitals in the great coastal area of South Carolina. Since this is a tourist area, we have people from all wakes of life here. My job as a nurse is to greet and assess all of the new employees that come for a job. And I do get to meet a lot of incredibly interesting people and just the little bit of time that I am with them, I could just about tell you their life story.

I am not an incredibly serious person, as you can tell by my writing, with the honest and outrageous things that I tell you. My writing just about sums me up, so just keep reading. I do like the fact that I am a humorous person and that there is never a dull moment around me. People don't tend to forget me, so I think that is a very positive trait. Whether the people that I work for like it or not doesn't really concern me much. I'm having fun with my life and with others, so if they want to sit and be serious all the time, *then good luck with that!* Just isn't my nature!

I love the people that work in and around my office. Most are not Southern by birth, just happen to be here by choice. We're a very diverse bunch.

Some are serious, but some are downright rowdy. I do include myself in that latter equation.

But I do believe that you have to have fun at work to survive. *Ain't no harm in having fun*; it makes the day go faster and more tolerable. I can't and never have been able to sit in an office all day, not talking or laughing with anyone, keeping to myself, and then going home. You might as well put me in a pine box now, *because it ain't gonna happen!*

My boss is an administrator, and I'll call him James, but to me he is just a good ole Southern boy in a fancy suit. He can be as professional as most and can be as witty as the best of them. We once had a team building day at one of the local parks for the human resources department, and I watched him jump up on a picnic table and dance and sing like some old movie star. Quite a character he is! He also has the same last name as my maiden name, so I swear we are kin to each other. He does appreciate my humor and certainly takes all that I can dish out. *Bless his heart!*

I tend to write humorous little stories or poems and send them to him over the company email, and to anyone else that I think has a sense of humor. Never mind that the *"computer police"* are always looking around, because I send them anyway. I do think *people in high places* should *"lighten up,"* so to speak, so this is just a sample of some of my creations and just some of my sassy observations. And this is just *all in fun*, so keep your pants on:

You need to be an administrator if you...
Like to wear all black suits, most of the time!

Your second job might be as a greeter at the local mortuary, or you're part of the local mob, you're in mourning, but no one knows! Or, honey, you have no fashion or color sense, and this is the best you can do! Or heck...you just like black! Stick with this chick, and I'll volunteer to take you on a shopping spree that you'll never forget! 'Cause Southern gals like color and plenty of it! Just ask anybody that has seen my shoes!

Like to wear stiletto heels
or very expensive shoes?

You have to have the most expensive 'cause you have an *image* to uphold. The rest of us don't think about your image, or what you have on your feet (unless it's interesting like a pair of leopard or zebra heels), but you think we do! *Shut my mouth!* And I bet if you asked someone to pick out the $300 pair of shoes versus the $29.99 special, I bet they couldn't tell.

You probably have bunions, hammertoes, and/or blisters, but you look good. Your dang feet hurt you all day, but this is just part of the job and your "image." And your podiatrist loves you! $$$ And that's why I think you have that *stressed* look on your face.

Always have the "look" on your face?

This can be misinterpreted as constipation by the other employees. *I don't misinterpret, I know!* You have ulcers, reflux, irritable bowel syndrome, and the "look" prevails. It's because of this image that you want us *little people* to see! And we're looking at you and snickering all the way down the hall. And it just might be caused by your expensive shoes or your dang job!

Drive the sportiest or most expensive cars in the parking lot?

Your other car is a ten-year-old pickup truck with dents on the side, but the staff is totally unaware of this! Or you don't have another car! Or it's a rental, but you're not telling. You want us *"little people"* to know that you make more money than us! *But, news-flash, we already know that!* And that car's trunk won't hold a week's worth of groceries or the family dog, so you have to go back home, change clothes, and put your dark sunglasses on, and get your pick up truck. Gotta keep the image going!

Live in the nicest and one of the most expensive neighborhoods?

You have no furniture, and you eat peanut butter, but you had to have that $750,000 house since you want to make a good impression. You haven't invited any-one inside yet. *And it certainly won't be me!* Don't know what you're going to do when you're asked to have that party. Better look up the rental furniture place. And I bet you have it on speed dial.

Carry a little black briefcase?

No one knows what's in it, but it might be a Sudoku book, crossword puzzles, and this month's current issue of *People Magazine* to entertain you at adminis-trative meetings. Lord *knows you aren't listening!* But you look important. (I bet it was a Kmart blue light special, and its 100% vinyl, but who cares anyway?) *Or there ain't a dang thing in it!* Remember President Truman; he carried record albums in his. Gotcha!

Have to carry your pocket phone/keyboard/internet with you everywhere?

People think you are taking notes, but you're really looking up the ballgame picks so you can text message your bookie to place a bet for you. Or you are looking up something on YouTube. *I could bet its YouTube!* I must agree that it's a lot more fun than any ole dang business meeting. That's also why you look like *deer in the headlights* when you're asked to comment at a meeting, 'cause you ain't listening. *So put the dang thing down!* Or at least put it where the CEO can't see it. That's my trick anyway!

You don't need to be an administrator if...

You like to wear comfortable, sporty clothes to work. Columbia, Liz, and Gap works for me! No dang tight waistbands to suck the life out of you.

You like to wear comfortable, affordable shoes so your feet don't hurt! No stiletto heels here! Go *Dansko!*

You like to smile, laugh, and give someone a hug or a pat on the back in the hall without anyone thinking anything about it! *"Cause you ain't an administrator, and you don't give a dang."*

Drive a modest car, because you can afford it! You also have another one at home. Lexus or BMW doesn't have a thing on you.

Live in a nice, but modest neighborhood, because

you like it! You have nice furniture and you eat steak two nights a week. Might even have a pool!

Carry a pocketbook instead of a briefcase! You're Southern, you know! Aigner or Liz is nice. They carry your lipstick a lot better too, and your nail file, your perfume, your...

You don't own a fancy phone; the basic one is just fine. You make calls to friends and family, seldom business. You can actually pay your phone bill off every month.

I'm just poking fun here, and I don't have anything against our fine administrative staff, and I mean that whole-heartedly! I just prefer not to be one, and so I have stayed on the *"back burner"* for years even though I probably have more healthcare experience than the majority of them. *You could say I like to watch from afar!* I have to admire people who want to take on a little more stress and responsibility than the rest of us, but I don't envy their workload, their ulcers, or their bills. But to help keep me sane and allow my family to be able to live with me, I have stayed out of the *limelight*. But I might be in it soon, due to spilling my guts here. *Or in the unemployment line!*

My channel-flipping husband is an administrator, and I swear he thrives on the stress of it all. If his normal day is not at least ten hours, it's not a *normal* day for him. Since he is so involved in what he does, I have to be the forty-hour a week one so that there can be some sort of balance in our household.

Getting back to my workplace, and my not so stressful world, I have some really funny Southern and "not so Southern" characters to introduce you to:

GO AHEAD...
TRY A NEW RECIPE *on* COMPANY

I love people, I love my relatives, And I love all of my friends. But I had rather take a jab in the back than cook for company! It is just a stressor that I have, and I just can't seem to get over it. When you say the word *"company,"* my heart starts accelerating, my stomach gets in knots, and let the stress begin. Go ahead and criticize if you want to, but about half of you are in this battle with me. If you're not, you've been reconditioned!

I always love it when my husband says, *"company is coming over,"* or "so and so is coming over!" *Good!* They are more than welcome to come over as long as I don't have to cook. Put out the Wheat Thins, the pimento cheese, the salted mixed nuts, Cokes, Pepsis, and the paper plates. Don't forget the napkins, so you can wipe your mouth, child! *Whew...I can handle that!* Just as long as they don't stay around until mealtime then I will be okay. But if it gets to that point, I'll be looking up the pizza delivery number. And I have got it on speed dial!

I probably exaggerated just a bit, but I do stress over having to cook for company. I always have! I am a good cook, but having to cook for someone else, well, I just predict disaster. I cook very simply for my family: meat, salad, a vegetable, maybe dessert or some type of bread. *Nothing fancy!* We usually eat straight from the stove or the microwave, sometimes on paper plates. My family would think that I had lost my ever-loving mind if I served them on the good china.

The good china, so to speak, comes out only on holidays usually. It's like having good jewelry that you never wear! Since I didn't get fine china when I got married, we inherited this from my husband's great aunt. I guess nobody else wanted it! *Why, shut my mouth!*

No...it's a beautiful pattern with gold around the edges and even came with some of those prissy coffee or teacups that hold about two mouthfuls. When I want coffee or hot tea, I want a mug! Prissy cups, in my opinion, went out with the dinosaurs! I would have a caffeine headache for sure if I only had that amount of coffee to drink every morning. Oh well, I shouldn't kick a gift horse in the mouth, and I do appreciate the seldom used china.

Getting back to company, I never know what to cook for them. I'm just afraid that the plain food that I cook will not be too impressive for company. (A Paula or a Rachel, I am not!) So...I go dig into the recipe books. *I must be crazy!* Most folks would never try out a new recipe on company; that's a cardinal rule. But I'm as nonconformist as I can be to tradition or anybody else's rules, so I am doomed from the get go!

I go and dig and dig and dig, and try to find something that will please me and I guess to please them too. I usually won't fix anything that has more than five ingredients, so I can't mess it up too bad. As long as I can taste it before I put it together, it will probably be okay.

So I find the perfect recipe, I put it together, and hope for the best. When it's finished, I take it out, hope it looks like the recipe, smells like I think it should, and I hope to the good Lord it tastes like it too! *But how do I know?* Because usually I've never made it before...what was I thinking?

The next step in making a new recipe for company is setting the proper table. (I am such a Chinet fan, that I think I have forgotten how.) Make sure china's in the right place, glass and bread plate are in the right place, but which side does the spoon, knife, and fork go, and do they pair up with one of them or go solo? Which side does the napkin go on? *But...does all of this horse hockey really matter?* I guess I don't think so! Little non-conformist me.

When people sit down to eat, do they mentally photograph the place setting to see if it is correct? Do they run out and tell all their friends if it isn't? Or do they enjoy the untested recipe that their hostess has prepared and savor all of the five ingredients that are in it? Do they appreciate the rarely used china that is before them? And do they see the results of the anti-anxiety medicine that the hostess had to take in order to get through this day? Do they? *Not a chance!*

Well, I have managed to survive every time I have had company over for some type of meal. It does involve a lot of thought, time, and preparation. At least 99% of it is mine! My channel-flipping husband tells me the news, unless it is my idea, and leaves the rest to me. *Bless his heart!* He watches me the whole time I am doing this too, and always asks to help me when it is time to sit down to eat! *Bless his heart again!* I do ask him to help on occasion by having him just stay out of my way. I tell him the television is anxiously waiting on him to push its buttons. *I should be shot for being so sassy!*

So the next time you have company, to save yourself a lot of stress and aggravation, just order pizza, pull out the Chinet, and have a good time! Throw those recipe books out the window. And if that doesn't work, take channel-flipping husband's credit card and go to the nicest restaurant that you can find on him! This will probably curb his desire to have a lot of company over for dinner any time soon!

Happy eating, ya'll, and make sure you have plenty of paper plates! And the number to the nearest pizzeria!

EVERYBODY HAS WEIRD RELATIVES ... OR *the* ONES YOU DON'T WANT TO SAY TOO MUCH ABOUT!

hat is the dang truth! I think everybody has relatives that might classify as weird, strange, ornery, a little peculiar, set in their ways, different, etc. Now say it ain't so! And some of their ways or habits we don't really want to advertise to the rest of the world. Not that we don't love them, 'cause we love our relatives regardless of how they act and what they say and do. And I'm talking about them here, not to make fun of them...but to let you know that you are not by yourself when you talk about your weird relatives or ones that don't exactly fit the mold of "norm." And to be quite honest, you probably don't go out and advertise that you're kin to them either, now do ya?

Everybody that I have ever met, or at least had any impact on me, always has stories to tell about their kinfolk or *sorta* kinfolk. Sorta kinfolk are relatives by marriage, and just for humor's sake, they, most of the time, have some of the funniest stories. I probably like their stories best because they are not in my gene pool! *Why, shut my mouth!*

Well, to get started, I will tell you about someone that was in my gene pool. She is on my mother's side of the family. My Aunt Linda or Linder as everyone mispronounced her name. No one ever said "aunt" either, as it should be pronounced, but "ain't." Bless her heart, she was one of the most opinionated women I have ever met or grew up with, but when it counted, she could be one of the most understanding and sincere.

Aunt Linda was someone that I grew up with. She helped to raise me, since my momma was so young when she had me. She was the first one in her family to go to college, and was an English major and eventually became a teacher. She did have one little *different* ambition when she was in high school though; she wanted to be a mortician.

"Why, I asked her one time?"

"Because I could make them look better than most."

But what kind of person goes around thinking that they could make dead people look better? I have a lot more things to think about and do, so I just don't give cosmetic makeovers of the deceased a serious thought. I don't mean that in an unkind way, just that my way of thinking is different.

She was also a little eccentric! I swear she wore the same clothes for forty years. When I was a young 'un, she wore Indian moccasins, white with silver buttons on the side, polyester pull-on pants, oversized shirts, and she always pin-curled her hair at night. Didn't they do that in the 50s? *I told you so!* She always tweezed her eyebrows so that they matched and were absolutely perfect. Then she would take a pencil and color them in, so to speak. I watched her do this many times. It's funny that you can remember details like that when you think about it.

She did like to eat weird things too! She ate ice like it was going out of style. Every time I saw her she was crunching on something. (You know they say it's a vitamin deficiency, but if you ate only ice, you'd be deficient too!) I really never saw her eat anything healthy except when my Nanny cooked it. She was funny about what she ate too. She didn't eat things that most people would eat, and combined things that really didn't go together. Like putting strange foods on my Nanny's biscuits, eating green hot pepper without anything to wash it down with, and any person borne and bred in the *sticks* knows not to do things like that.

Strange pets were also one of her traits. One time she had a pet goat named Ginger in the backyard. She kept her in a chain-link fence with a shed for a goat house that looked like a small outhouse. That was the fattest goat I had ever seen. I would have put it to work cutting the grass and eating weeds like most goats do. No, she just kept her in a pen and finally gave her away. That was a bad decision. I would have kept that goat as a lawnmower and saved myself some money and labor!

She also had about ten feral cats, maybe more, that she fed and kept outside. She also had one inside that looked like a lynx and another one that was a large, grey Persian. I think I used to be afraid of her cats since the lynx used to hiss at me and look at me with wild eyes, and the Persian used to bite me every chance she got. *Dang felines!*

Dressing up was also not Linda's virtue, and she would wear her curlers a lot, especially to Sunday dinner. They were the bristle type that only older ladies wear nowadays, and would cling to the top of her head in a neat little row. With, I might add, those pink plastic pins that you would hold them on with. *Ouch!* And she had the pin curls on the end. I think sometimes they pulled your hair so tight that it rearranged your brain cells. At least I thought so when I used to wear them. *What a painful thing it was!*

Getting back to not dressing up, she also didn't like to wear shoes a lot. I saw her bare feet in rain, sleet, and snow. One Christmas she came down to my Nanny's for dinner, and she was in her bare feet. But give her credit, her toenails were always polished, and I never saw a crack in her heels. I never knew her to catch a cold or get sick like a lot of other folks. I guess her barefoot habit didn't hurt her none! But, I guess if most of your footwear were Indian moccasins, you couldn't be all wrong. Isn't that what the Indians wore, and I bet they weren't sick a lot.

Linda was a good kindergarten teacher, and she did this for many years. After that she worked for the Council on Aging and helped the elderly. Then she decided that she wanted to be a deputy police officer. Bless her soul, she would go out with another officer at night and volunteer her time to jump in the middle of fights, domestic disputes, etc., you name it. I forgot to tell you that she was also a big woman, not a tall woman, but as big as a football player, once upon a time. She wasn't afraid of anything and told you so a lot! Maybe that's where some of my sassiness started?

Always having an opinion about everything, whether right or wrong, people didn't seem to want to argue with her except her husband. Most of us just rolled our eyes and pretended not to hear her. You couldn't help but hear her though, since she was the loudest one in the house, and the house was small.

But, after all this, Aunt Linda was the entertaining one of the bunch! She had a cackle that could be heard around the neighborhood, and when she got mad, a voice that carried too. Anyone that ever met her did wonder about her. She left no stone unturned or anything unsaid. You knew just where she stood, whether you wanted to or not!

I loved my aunt though! And I say loved. She died at the age of sixty-seven from a year-long battle with cancer. Eccentric as she was, I will never forget her little quirks and remember them often. A colorful character she was, and though a little different sometimes, I smile when I think of her and will miss her always.

I do have some other relatives that I'd like to mention. This is the story of my two uncles Wayne and Joseph, but not their real names of course. They are on my daddy's side of the family, but he is not anything like these two. I guess those genetics did not get to him.

Uncle Wayne was in the military most of my young life, so I didn't get to know him very well. He had a strange laugh and laughed about everything. I would say, "Hello," and he would say, "Hey Kathleen," and start laughing. That was a little strange to me, or was I that funny looking? He seemed to always be accompanied by a glass with ice and brown liquid in it, so I guess that is where some of that laughter originated. I do remember him sitting on a bar stool a lot, but you know kids remember everything and remember it vividly. *At least this little girl did!*

I was a little afraid of him too, and I used to stay by my Grandma when he was around. I don't think he liked kids much, 'cause he never really talked to me then and really didn't talk to me much when I got older. My Momma was not fond of *that brown liquid*, so she would take me home shortly after he came to visit. We never had any of that stuff in our house, and Southern Baptists and my family didn't allow it.

I probably shouldn't tell stories like this, but it's the truth. *When you're a kid you notice everything and tell it too!* Uncle Wayne did stay in the house a lot, and they used to have a lot of bottles on the bar. Grandma kept them put away most of the time, until Uncle Wayne or some of my other aunts and uncles would come to visit. Never did see them out any other time, so when I did I knew company was coming, and the home atmosphere would change; lots of talking, laughing, and calling me by the wrong name.

Joseph, or Uncle Joseph as I used to call him, was a little strange too. I should *shut my mouth*, but this is part of the story. He was the oldest of his brothers and sisters, and they told a story about him. They said that when he was a young boy he got hit in the head, and that is why he was the way he was. He always had a *funny* look in his eyes, so I guess that explains it.

Uncle Joseph used to call me "Cappie" and would put that name on all of my Christmas presents. I do not have the foggiest idea where he got that name from. All of my life people making up names to call me. He liked to drink out of the same bottles that the rest of the family liked to drink out of at special times, but usually his "special" time was all the time. He always had a glass out, and I don't ever remember him not slurring his speech a little bit. *Must be the head hitting thing?*

I didn't stay around my uncles very much when they came to visit when I was little. And I didn't see them very much when I became an adult either. Makes a difference who raises you and who spends time with you when you are growing up; if people are absent during that time, you're not really close to them when you're all grown up. I'm getting a little sentimental here, so don't mind me. *But it's the dang truth!* And this book is about the truth, so I do tend to tell it all.

Not much else to say about them. They both died in their sixties, I think both from heart conditions. They were both a little like my grandfather "Grampy" and didn't see the use in taking modern medicine. Sometimes men can be stubborn about taking care of themselves, and my uncles and my grandfather were prime examples. I did try to talk to them once or twice, but I think it fell on deaf ears. But if they couldn't remember my right name, how the heck would they remember anything else. *Shut my mouth!*

I don't want to identify this next relative, but she is not genetically linked. She is one of the funniest and naive women that I have ever met in my life, and has been in my family for a long time. Her *normal* life is a funny story and well worth the time to write about it.

Everybody does get a *kick* out of her, especially my children and they love to tell what her current *"hair brain"* idea is. But don't blame them; her husband is the one that starts the *fireworks!* So point fingers in his direction, but all of us do drill him as soon as we see him, to tell us what she has been up to, bought, given away, wrecked, said, and I could go on and on!

Have you ever, *of course you have,* seen a picture of one of those famous blondes, like Miss Marilyn? Well this is my relative, shorter perhaps, but just as childlike. The things that come out of her mouth sometimes make absolutely no sense. You see, she has to take several different medicines because she has a couple of health problems (I'm exaggerating a little bit here), but some of them must have odd side effects and she can't control her talking sometimes. She is absolutely hysterical once she gets going. *Whew!* I don't know how she does it!

I am probably going to get a smack when this relative recognizes her bio here, but I can't resist telling you some of the *"cock a mania"* things she has done since I have known her. Heck, her husband wanted to write them down too. She might think I am doing this to be mean, but I'm really not! My whole family thinks she is hysterical, and the things that she does are too funny *not* to share, so here goes:

1) Burnt her new kitchen up when grease caught fire on the stove, and she ran out of the house instead of putting a lid on it. We do tell her to *"put a lid on it"* a lot, but it goes way over her head. *Shut my mouth!*

2) Calls the famous designer Wera Lang instead of by the proper name. Medication brought that on, I bet!

3) Buys clothes without trying them on, and so she can't wear them when she gets them home. Never takes

them back to the store, but gives them away or throws them in the dumpster. A very lucky sanitation crew!

4) Buys a new sofa every Christmas and new furniture throughout the year. It's not that there is anything wrong with the old one; she just gets tired of it. *Who does that?* She has bought enough furniture to give away that she has furnished all of her family's houses.

5) Redecorates her house at least once a month and can't leave anything in its place for more than a day or two. Throws these away too. Has helped to furnish my house! (And I might be exaggerating a little bit here.)

6) Goes to a fine restaurant, orders T-bone steak, and when she is finished picks up the bone with both hands and gnaws on it 'til she picks it clean. Grease and bone are all over her face. That's why they give her an extra handi wipe at the door! This might be a little exaggeration, but I couldn't resist telling you about it, and I told her so!

7) Dyes her hair on a regular basis to match the blonde bombshell look, but she says it's natural. *Then why the heck are all those hair color boxes in the cabinet?* Now...I didn't go snooping in her cabinets, but that's my hypothesis. And that's a very big word for a Southern belle.

8) Buys little gifts, leaves the price tags on, and wraps them up in large, pricey boxes. *Why...thank you for this great box!* I am still using some of them that I've saved to this day, plus the ribbon, and she makes fun of me.

9) Wears a full-length mink coat (no faux here) to walk on the beach in the winter. Accompanied by blue jeans and white Ked tennis shoes! "It's my coat and it's warm, and I'm going to wear it!" she says. *But who's going to stop her?* Maybe a game warden!

10) Last but not least, she loses ten pounds every month, or so she says. By this time she should be down to weighing about thirty pounds, but who's counting?

I did exaggerate a little, maybe a lot, but this gal is a laugh a minute, but none of us take her too seriously. I don't think my relative that married her does either. She is very entertaining, and once she gets started and has an audience, there's never a dull moment. But we don't dare tell anyone else for fear that they will think we are a little strange. At least one of us is! *Why, shut my mouth, again and again!*

Relatives are a gift and we love them, but we don't have to like everything they say and do. LORD knows we try to tolerate! And I guess as unreasonable or wacky as they may be, our relationships with them also impact our relationships with ourselves. They are part of who we are, good or bad.

But Southerners are good at trying to tolerate these relatives and know when to leave before they smack somebody on the head. *You know I'm right!* But God bless my many family members however different and intolerable they may be, but I realize I am not alone and that everybody has at least one relative they'd like to shove in the closet and forget about. Or maybe a few!

Now say amen to that and pray they don't have to take a drug test!

CONTINUING...
GROWING UP SOUTHERN!

The last time you and I talked about my childhood, I told you about my family. I had a lot of family members growing up, and they were all around me. I had three sets of grandparents and lots of aunts, uncles, cousins, and in-laws; so many family members, and we did a lot of things together. Holidays like Christmas, Thanksgiving, and Easter, weddings, funerals, new babies, birthdays, family reunions, graduations, and things like *"just coming to town to visit"* gatherings. We were always together.

I had one brother growing up, but by the time it was all over, I had inherited three stepsisters and one stepbrother. My Momma only had one sister growing up, and my Daddy had four brothers and one sister, so he was in a family of eight. (There would have been a family of ten, but he lost two of his siblings as infants.) My grandmother Nanny grew up with three sisters and two brothers. My Grand Daddy Paul had two brothers and two sisters. As you see, we had rather large families, so that was the reason for so many relatives.

It's kinda nice having so many relatives! You never run out of conversation and you never run out of food!

Whew! Makes my mouth water now to think about the feasts we would have. If you've ever been to anything that is sponsored by a Southern family, it will most definitely be surrounded by food. And it usually won't be the "box type" either, 'cause Southern women know how to cook and how to make plenty of it. *Mm…mm…* and pass the fried chicken!

Southern people know how to eat too! Must definitely be in their genes! When I was growing up, most of the women that I knew were never skinny. They had *"plenty of meat on their bones,"* as my Nanny used to say. They were excellent cooks and always had something tasty for you to try. Even today, I can still remember going at least every day to my Nanny's for something to eat. *And you know what?* She always had something! I can't remember my grandmother's stove ever being without something on it, even if it was just a biscuit or a piece of pie.

Nanny was an excellent old Southern-style cook. *Have you ever heard of blackberry dumplings?* One of the best things I have ever tasted in my whole life! (And I'll even share that with you in the back of this book!) I think she made this recipe up, but it was so dang good. Hand cut, long dumplings that she had made from scratch, fresh blackberries in them that she had picked from the patches herself, and baked in a casserole dish. *Yum!* I can still taste it and sad that I probably won't ever again!

Nanny loved to pick blackberries! And I know 'cause I went with her a time or two. She could spy a blackberry patch a mile away! A crying shame, that the land is so developed now that wild patches don't really exist anymore. I might see one here and there, once in a while, but the plants are low to the ground, and the berries don't look like what she used to pick. The patches that Nanny would go in would be up over her waist, and in she would go!

I remember her going in there with her dress and her apron on, and usually a big pan to put her blackberries in. She never wore pants, at least not at that time of my life, so she didn't have on anything to really keep her from getting scratched by the briars. *And boy did those plants have plenty of them.* If you wanted to torture somebody, you could just throw them in the blackberry briars!

Nanny didn't seem to mind picking blackberries, and I think she was the only family member that did it too, except for little me that liked to hold the pan for her. She didn't seem to be too scared of snakes, since that didn't stop her. I was always looking around for them, and I think I would have *wet my pants* if I had seen one! To this day I will run from a snake; I won't harm it, just run!

Nanny put a lot of love in whatever she did for her family, and cooking is what she did best. Have you ever heard of anyone going into a briar patch to get fresh berries for their family? She wasn't really getting them for herself, but so she could make her wonderful blackberry dumplings that I told you about, also jams and jellies. I don't ever remember her eating any of them, because the family liked them so much, and she would rather see you enjoy eating something than eating it herself.

My momma was and is a great cook too! Just like my Nanny, only a little different. We always had fully homemade meals when I was growing up with all the fixin's. My Daddy liked large meals, and I don't remember many small ones. He was a big man when I was little and had a very big appetite. He worked hard too in the paper mill, and he was hungry when he got home from work. Momma always said that a woman should keep herself fixed up and make sure there was food on the table when your husband comes home from work. That's the old Southern way, and I did think about it a lot when I was growing up and tried to adopt her ways of being a grown woman, such as cooking and cleaning. We have since changed our opinions a little bit (and I am decelerating this statement), since I am now a grown woman and think that *slavery* went out a long time ago! *Shut my mouth!*

Now let's get back to my nice little story, before I get my *feathers* ruffled. Momma is a good cook to this day, but doesn't cook much the good ole Southern style unless it is a holiday or something. Me neither, but I still love it to pieces.

Hidden facts like cholesterol and triglycerides have kept me from eating like a true Southerner, and also a little thing or rather a big thing like cellulite. *Just look in the rear view mirror, honey. Ouch!*

But you know what? My relatives, while I was growing up, didn't worry about that kind of stuff. I guess there weren't any machines to measure it back then, if there were, the doctors didn't talk about it. They just kept on eating the fried chicken and the biscuits and molasses till they were good and ready to stop! When they finally did stop, it was belly up on the couch for a nap for a few hours, and ha, back then there wasn't such a thing as a channel changer. If they had to change the channel, they had to get off of their butts and do it manually. Probably lost weight doing that too! Maybe that's what's wrong with our men today. *Oops...getting off on a tangent again!* Must be that ingrained memory stuff!

I suppose you can guess with that last paragraph that I was talking about the *"men folks,"* as my Nanny used to say. The *"women folks,"* during this belly up time, were usually in the kitchen doing the dishes. And we didn't have a dishwasher back then, and it was all done by, you guessed it, just your plain ole hands. All of them, including me, would stand around and all would pitch in to stack and wash those dishes. Had to rake out all of what was left on them, rinse them off and stack them up. Then take everything out of the sink, fill it up with soap and water (had to be hot), and one by one put the dishes in and wash them. Rinse them off and put them in a dish drainer, unless you were lucky enough for someone to want to dry them. Then they would put them away for you.

We didn't use Playtex gloves then, and there wasn't a piece of Chinet in the house. *How did we ever survive?* And everybody pitched in to help, and you didn't sneak off and go watch television with the men folks either. You stayed in the kitchen with the women until all the dishes were done and the food was put away. Or you got a tongue-lashing from my momma or the evil eye. And you didn't want either one!

My momma was a big believer in children helping out in the house, having chores, minding their manners, and knowing when to be quiet. She certainly jerked me up a time or two in my childhood for not doing the above. She was big on discipline too and didn't think that children should misbehave. She's still a believer in all of it now, and I guess I can say that I am right there with her. There's nothing better in my opinion than a well-mannered child, and the parents of that child should be very proud. A lot of hard work goes into teaching a child to behave, and I know my momma worked hard to try to get us to be the best that we could be.

We weren't bad children, my brother and me, but our grandparents spoiled us terribly. Especially me, since I was the oldest. I got to have them all to myself for five years before anybody else came along. I got to ride between them in the front seat of the car without a seat belt and stand up in the seat; never did fall that I know of. I sometimes would climb in the back seat, lay down in the back window when cars actually had them, and wave at all the cars that came by or rode on my Grand Daddy Paul's bumper. I got to go to the *"dime store"* with Nanny and get something every time we'd go in. Usually it was a box of cough drops, and don't ask me why! I ate them like candy, but I don't think they were like they are today, full of strong ingredients and such.

I would drink coffee at the table with them and put too much sugar and *Cremora* in it. Loved the stuff though! We would have *"pop"* weenies and huge dill pickles from the Army commissary since Grand Daddy Paul was in the reserves. If you have never had a pop weenie, you have missed a treat. All of these weenies were strung together, and they would pop when you tried to bend them. They would also come wrapped up in white paper, something that not many butchers do today.

The pickles were great too, and I ate them until I

couldn't eat anymore. I still love pickles to this day, and I can still eat a jar of kosher baby dills without batting an eye.

I was the *"barefoot contessa"* back then too and never liked to wear shoes. My little feet were always dirty, and I always had to wash them off before I went to bed. Mind you, I did take a bath, not a shower, but my feet didn't get clean for some reason. If I took a bath at Nanny and Grand Daddy Paul's, I had to boil the water first on the stove and pour it in the bathtub just like I told you. You had about ten to fifteen minutes before the water got ice cold, and you had to wash quickly!

This didn't seem to bother them though, 'cause they did it for years. I guess when you grow up with next to nothing, anything that was better than you had is a blessing. Nanny grew up in a small house with a lot of children and had to share everything, and Grand Daddy Paul really didn't ever mention much of a home, so this was probably just fine for him. They were just simple people that didn't need much and didn't ask for anything either. Having a roof over their head, enough food to eat, savings in the bank and a secure job were the important things to them. And a relationship with God ruled over all else!

Nanny and Grand Daddy Paul didn't go to church that much, but they still talked about the Bible often and watched it on television. Nanny had bad legs and Paul had a bad back, so sitting in the hard, wooden church pews was a little uncomfortable. Both of them were good people, put their family first before themselves, and there was never anything that we asked of them that they wouldn't do for us. I just wish that we could have done more for them.

Well, I'm getting too sentimental here, maybe not, but I loved my grandparents. I love my parents too, they don't live very close, but we keep in touch as much as we can. Families are to be cherished, to make memories, and to pass these memories and experiences on to our children, whether they want to listen are not. And that *not listening thang* seems to be common among the young people.

Both of my children live with my husband and me now, and this is the second time around again! Never say, *"You can't go home again,"* 'cause they did. They have been fun to have around though, and there is never a dull moment around here with this bunch in the house. We get along well for the most part, and I try to let all of us share in the household responsibilities. But if I have worked all day, my feet are tired, my head hurts, I am aggravated, and you are going to take your life in your hands if you ask me what's for dinner. And my reply will be to you: a swat upside the head with my pocketbook, an evil eye (genetically maintained), and I am going straight to my room for a *"belly up"* nap! Ain't that just like a Southern belle with an attitude?

Proud of it, ya'll! Now learn to cook! Or at least learn how to fend for yourself, 'cause you can't depend on anybody else except the good LORD! And He ain't gonna cook for you either, 'cause that is not in His contract, so get off your duff!

IN DEFENSE
of MY SASSINESS ...

It got to thinking about it, like I always do, and I bet a lot of you wonder where I get some of my *cock a mania* stories? Well, as I have said before, my writings are from true-life experiences, but I do tend to stretch the truth just a little from time to time. You have to, to make it a little more humorous. But they aren't fiction by any means, 'cause real life makes the best stories, don't you think?

I tend to write about my family a lot, 'cause we all live together in a little beach house, but it's home, and we all do what we can to make it work. My children are grown, but one is still going to college and one is working and trying to find themselves. But just because they are grown doesn't mean that you stop being a momma and that they automatically become adults and start doing for themselves. It would be *"in my dreams"* if they did, and I guess they will probably stay right here, until they are able to make it and set up their own household.

It's funny, but when I go to my own momma's house, she is still the mother and I am the child, and I have not lived with her for over thirty years. That's a funny thing, and I guess all of us are that way to an extent. My husband was that way with his parents until they died. And his parents always treated him like *my child*, not in a hovering way, but lovingly.

I adore my husband and my children, even though I do make fun of some of the crazy things that they do. We're just a normal family; some have even called us Ozzie and Harriett minus the pearls and the pumps at breakfast. Ah … but that's another story!

Since I am very outspoken, and a lot of people have told me this, I think I say things that a lot of women have been thinking for years but *don't dare say it!* I say things sometimes on an impulse, and like my friend Carol says, ask for forgiveness later! I never mean any harm by what I say; I just speak the truth and hope not too many people take offense to it. But I guess if you were too offended, you wouldn't be reading my book. And I do thank you for that!

But everyday life is hysterical if you sit back and really think about what people do from day to day. Sometimes I don't even know where my ideas come from; I do give the LORD credit since He gave me the ability to start writing in this middle-age chapter of my life. I have never written in my life except for papers in school, and all of a sudden I have this knack for it, and can't seem to write enough. I get ideas at the craziest times of day, like in the morning when I'm putting on my face for the day, and that does take some time, taking the dog for a walk, and today when I was blowing off the pollen in the driveway. *So what's up with that?*

I do write a lot about my husband, and at first he seemed a little offended by my humor. But he is one funny man and doesn't have a clue that his habits are downright hysterical at times. But when I talk to other women, their husband's have a lot of the same habits. Most of the time, though, we don't draw attention to them, because they get very defensive, pout, and act like you have just cut them to the core. And when my husband read some of the stuff in my first book, he said, "Why are you telling that?"

I just replied "That's humor, honey!"

"Well I don't see any humor in it."

They just don't understand, and that's why my audience is mostly women.

I'm not a women's libber or anything, maybe a tad, and definitely not a bra burner, 'cause Lord knows I need mine, at least in this stage of the game. I would dang near scare somebody to death if I didn't wear one. I just believe that marriage is a partnership, and that everything in it should be shared. Housework, yard work, laundry, trash, dog and cat responsibilities, grocery shopping, picking up, etc. And throw the kids in there if they live in your house and put their feet under your table. *Amen!*

I don't abuse my husband by any means, but as I said, I probably am saying things that women have been thinking for years. My momma took care of my daddy when they were married, and my Nanny took care of Grand Daddy Paul. It's a woman thing, and it is in the Bible, but I do believe it can be a two-way street. A long time ago women didn't work outside the home, so they were the sole caretakers. And back in Bible times, women didn't work outside the home either, 'cause if they did, Moses or David might have been asked to take their own loin cloths and robes down to the river and wash them. Nah, you say, but I bet they just might have.

We don't really know what women have thought all these years, but I can take a pretty wild guess. *They just didn't say it!*

I take care of my family, and they better not beg to differ. They really have it made. I was not born a hard worker, but I became one, and I can run circles around anybody else that lives here. Plus I try to exercise and take care of myself too. I used to put myself on the back burner, but not anymore. As you get older, you need to take care of yourself, or things will start to sag, gravity will take over, and you will not be happy. *But that is another chapter!*

And growing up in a good ole Southern family helped make me the way I am too! *But doesn't everyone's family?* I had a lot of outspoken women to have for role models, so I guess I get it honest. I love the movie "Gone with the Wind," and maybe I'm a little bit like Scarlett, but not the whole package. I'm certainly not a Mellie or Melanie! Today she would be called a *doormat,* and that is definitely not what I am about.

So girls, and maybe a guy or two, just bear with me. I just want you to laugh and have fun while reading this book and maybe think about normal everyday things just a little bit differently. 'Cause laughter is a blessing, and we should do it every day and often and shouldn't care who is around. *Maybe you'll rub off on them!* Especially on those *constipated* people in our lives that just can't seem to get it! If you don't remember what a constipated person is, it's those people that can't have fun with their lives and are way too serious for me. Probably for you too, if you like humor.

Happy reading, ya'll, and keep finding the humor and sassiness in every situation, 'cause life is too short to be too serious! Besides, your facial muscles exert too much energy being serious, and this cause wrinkles, and those cause...

AIN'T NO ORDER IN *this* COURTROOM!

Not that I have been inside a courtroom many times in my life, but I have had my "not so fair" share. *Just for minor traffic tickets, so don't get all smirky!* Ok, maybe true traffic court once, but I'm not counting it!

I'm not going to name this town, but I was quite surprised by what I saw when I walked in or rather before I walked in. I had only been to a courtroom once in my life and it was to attend jury duty. Never did get picked to do it though, 'cause who in their right judicial mind is going to pick a nurse on a medical case? I guess we know too dang much, plus if we know the defendant by first name, that works as a strike against us too. *Lucky me!*

Well, I guess I thought this would be some *high falootin'* courtroom since it was in the state of North Carolina right over the county line, but I'm still not telling! You know, North Carolina is known for their strict traffic laws, and they seem to like to belittle ole South Carolina a bit. Or rather they have the same laws, just try to make them look fancier than ours by their higher tickets, more points, and longer lock-ups. But I do respect that! Hey, it seems to work for them!

The morning that I was supposed to go to court, I got dressed to the hilt! Nice suit, not black but with a little color, jewelry, makeup and hair neat, even had a matching pocketbook and shoes. I was dressed for seriousness. I thought if anything the judge would take one look at me and decide that I was too classy to have a ticket, and he just might drop it altogether. I was in for a big surprise and whom was I kidding?

I drove up to the courthouse, circled the block about five times, almost driving into the exit of a bank, up on the curb, and finally found a place to park my car. Why do they make it so dang difficult to get in here? Must be part of the punishment.

So I took my pocketbook and walked, in my matching shoes, to the courthouse entrance; me and about two hundred other people at the same time. Didn't realize that I had to be stripped and searched to get in this building. Just like the airport!

By the time it was my turn to get stripped and searched, I got in the line that said "those with handbags." A pocketbook was a handbag in my opinion, so I put it on the little conveyor belt like I was supposed to. And I also put my newspaper, my Sudoku book, my keys, and my lipstick.

"Ma'am, just your pocketbook please!"

I really didn't pay attention at first.

"Ma'am, you're holding up the line, just your pocketbook!"

"Oh, sorry." And proceeded to take the rest of the stuff off of the conveyor belt.

Grouchy policeman talking to me like that just 'cause he can. Knows good and well that I can't swat him in here, but he can't stop me from giving him the evil eye. *And I did!* And I had good eyeliner on too!

Got through that *cotton pickin'* line, took my pocketbook, turned left, and weaved through the people to get to the stairwell. But not before stopping at the bathroom to freshen my lipstick and take care of business. That initial greeting had got me all in a fluster.

After I finished, I went upstairs and went to the waiting area before the actual courtroom opened. Every kind of person known to man was in there. I don't care about height, weight, or race, but the clothing on some of those people was hysterical! I had tried to dress the best that I could to make a good impression, and hopefully to help my case, but by the looks of some of those people, they were going to jail! No ifs, ands, or buts! *To jail, baby!*

Hats turned around backwards, sloppy oversized jeans, big t shirts that could fit two people in them, underwear showing, picks in their hair, stiletto heels, short skirts, low cut blouses, too much dang makeup, and piercings in some places that shouldn't be pierced. Some people looked like they had just crawled out of bed. And I had spent at least an hour or two getting ready. *So what's up with these people?* I think they were trying to make a statement at the wrong time.

I scanned the room and found a place to sit down. This room was already packed, and they continued to try to pack more in. I kept looking around the room, and I do remember a girl with a ton of makeup and high teased hair, short skirt, low cut blouse, to say the least, but very inappropriate looking. We'll just call her Hoochie for starters.

When I saw Hoochie, I thought to myself, *She prob-*

ably won't be back on the streets for a while! Ha…was that an understatement! Not that I was staring at her or nothing (yes I was), but there wasn't a whole lot to do in that room, and she was the most interesting person that I saw. Plus, I was thinking about how much time she might have to serve for her sins!

After sitting in the *"sardine can"* for a few minutes, they finally opened the door to the courtroom, and we all went in like we were going to a football game. I decided to sit on the back row so I could see everybody, since I wasn't so sure about this place. Some very interesting characters were coming in there, and I didn't want to miss nothing. Plus I don't like to have my back turned to the uncertain.

If you know anything about a courtroom, there is a bench or raised seat for the judge in the center, and tables in front on each side for the attorneys, clients, district attorney, and whoever is privileged to sit there. On the far right and left sides against the wall might be a place for a jury, or in this case, the traffic cops. And sitting to the right of the judge's seat was a place for the clerk of court. I hope I explained it a little, since I don't know the fancy names for any of them. Like I said, I am no expert at courtrooms, so you have to take what you can get! It's just a big room like it looks on television, all important though, and a little scary.

We sat there for about an hour before the judge finally got into the courtroom. *Guess he's probably just like a doctor and can never be on time.* Behind him came the clerk of court, and bless my sweet britches, it was Hoochie, and I almost fell off of my seat. *What in God's name were they thinking?* A fine courtroom such as this, and you put someone up there like that to represent the fine state of North Carolina! *I be dern!* I guess that means there's hope for anybody! Maybe for me in getting out of this ticket.

After I got my composure back, I looked around the room to see what other crazy things I could find. Traffic cops to the right, lawyers and district attorney in the middle, Hoochie to the left, and the *"be quiet"* deputies to the far left. The cops on the right seemed to be having a good ole conversation, because I heard them laugh more than once. They were talking so loud at one point the judge stopped what he was doing, looked in their direction as not to interrupt their conversation, and they finally stopped. I couldn't believe it! *Who is in charge here?*

He ain't no Judge Judy, who would have put their little loud butts right out the door. *Love that woman!* Well, this judge was not Judy, and every once in a while he still had to stop. *Ain't no respect, even for a judge here!* I kinda felt sorry for him too. Dang cops taking advantage of him. Wondered if he might want to borrow my pocketbook and give them a good swat or two? Or I could volunteer for the job. Does volunteer work reduce your fine?

On the far left of the room were the "order in the court" deputies, and when we came in they told everyone to be quiet, take your hats off, turn your cell phones off, ya da ya da ya da. I wasn't planning on talking to anyone, turned my cell phone off, and sat with my hands folded in my lap. I would frequently reach in my pocketbook and pull out a granola bite when the deputies weren't looking. "No eating or drinking in the courtroom!" and I know they weren't talking to me. *Munch, munch!* Don't they know you get hungry having to sit in here?

One big dude came in with a hat on, and he was loudly told to take it off. Cell phones continued to chime from time to time and people had their own independent conversations going on. Several, well about twenty-five people came in late, which ticked me off. If they tell you to be here at nine a.m., then you should be here at nine a.m. That just sends a message to the judge that you wanted to sleep in. I sure didn't get to sleep in; came here about thirty minutes early. *Don't let me get on my soapbox!*

As I continued to sit there and wait my turn, I watched the "attorney party" in the front. They were carrying on conversations, laughing, huddling, and several times the judge had to stop and wait for them to be quiet. *What's up with that?* Can't he just order the "be quiet" deputies to handcuff all the talkers and just carry them on out of there? No cops, no attorneys, everybody go home with a slap on the wrist and call it a day. Works for me, and just might work for the judge.

Well, my name was finally called, I walked up to the bench, listened to what the good judge had to say, said, "Yes, your honor," and was on my way to see Hoochie. She just looked at me with those big fake eyelashes of hers and proceeded to write out my receipt. It was all I could do to stand there with a straight face while her long pink acrylic nails went to work. It's a wonder she could type, much less hold a pencil. I continued to ask myself, *what is the world coming to?* And why is she wearing that shade of pink nail polish?

I finished with Hoochie, was excused, then proceeded to leave the courtroom through the double doors, down the stairs, by some more cops, through the revolving doors, and out into the world again. Thank goodness, and I hope I won't ever have to go through that again. All those dang people in that courtroom made me nervous, and I couldn't even eat (ha!) or sip a cold drink while I was sitting there. Not a very Southern hospitable place. Plus they hired Hoochie as their clerk of court. *Ain't never gonna forget that!* And she even had the wrong shade of pink on her nails. Didn't exactly match her outfit either; her shoes and accessories could have been given a little work too. And a Southern belle always notices that.

I told my husband that I shouldn't have tried to drive backwards and then managed to hit a tree, the tree fell and hit the neighbor's car, which pushed into the house, caused some damage to it by leaving a hole in the door, their prize winning dog got out and ran off to a neighbor's, chased a cat up a tree, and it wouldn't come down, had to call the fire department, and the fire truck made so much noise that it caused another neighbor to have a heart attack, so we called the ambulance. Had you going, didn't I? I really did go to the courthouse for a ticket, but I had to add a little more to spice it up.

Now, just so you know, I don't have a thing against our fine judicial system. I have some relatives that are part of it, one is even a judge himself, and I am very proud of them. But they are my relatives, and I know *darn tootin'* that they wouldn't have such a thing going on in their courtroom. In fact, I told the relative that's a soon to be judge about it, and he gave me the strangest look. Look, heck, more like his face turned inside out!

And then there was the hiring of Hoochie to represent them. Just let me have her for a day or two, and I could make a respectable Southern lady out of her! Might take a lot of soap and water or a sand blaster, but we'd get there. She made that courtroom look ridiculous and the judge to look like a *"pimp."* Sorry, but I do get carried away sometimes and I do tell it like I see it.

So the next time you have to go to traffic court and, honey child, I hope you don't, don't bother getting too dressed up. Heck, half the town wears pants that are too long and advertise for their underwear company. And if you're lucky enough to look like Hoochie, you just might get job in the courthouse and not have to pay your ticket, or anything else for that matter.

Now fancy that and *shut my mouth!* At least for a little while, but only maybe.

DON'T TAKE MY HUSBAND *to* A MEXICAN RESTAURANT, EVER!

My daughter Kelli and I love to eat Mexican food! *Absolutely love it!* When they bring the salsa bowl to the table with fresh hot corn chips, we nearly dive into it. Plus we usually order another bowl of hot cheese dip to go with all of this, and I want to stick my fingers in the bowl it is so good! But that wouldn't be ladylike, so I just run my finger around the edge of the bowl where the cheese drips. Yum! *Ain't nobody lookin' no way!*

My son Josh also likes it, Mexican food that is, and most of the time he will join us too. Usually it's just me and the kids, and that is fine. I don't have to cook for anyone, it's the night before I have to get up at 5a.m. since I do have a day job, so I can just eat and let somebody else clean up the mess if we do happen to leave a crumb or two. *Where's my husband?* He is usually at a sports event, so I take advantage of him not being home and take the kids out to eat.

Well, my husband decided that the last time we went to this particular restaurant that he would join us. *I really couldn't understand why?* He was supposed to be at a ballgame, swears he will never eat any more Mexican food, and definitely not there, so why was he coming? He just told me last night that he would not be going there. So I had planned for just one child, and I to go and get some good 'ole Mexican food, since the other child was busy, but my husband was on his way!

Kelli and I went to the restaurant together, and my husband would be right behind us. We got seated in about one minute, and my husband soon followed. Kelli and I had already looked at the menu while we were waiting, and contemplated what we would be eating. The usual, chicken fajita quesadillas every time, since it is our favorite.

Kelli and I were ready to order when he sat down, but he started up a conversation, so it took him a while to open the menu. The waiter came over to our table and quickly presented us with a big bowl of those chips and salsa. All three of us dove in, and my husband still had not opened his menu.

The waiter came back to the table and took our drink order: two sweet teas for the Southern belles and one diet Coke for my husband, the Southern gentleman. He came back with the drinks, put them down, and my husband still had not opened his menu. I gently nudged him, no elbow wallop yet and said, "Hon, you need to decide what you want to eat." So he finally opened his menu and said, "Can I just eat tacos?" I agreed and thought that was the end of it.

He kept looking and flipping, looking and flipping that menu. The waiter came again to the table and he still hadn't made up his mind.

"I thought you were going to eat tacos?" I asked.

"What's a burrito, and does it have beans in it?"

"Yes Hon."

"Well what's an enchilada and does it have beans in it? Meat?"

"No, not unless you want that in it. I thought you wanted tacos?"

"What's a chalupa? And does it have beans in it? What about a chile relleno? Does it have beans in it?"

"No Hon, I thought you just wanted the tacos?"

I was thinking to myself, *if he asks one more question I am going to scream at the top of my lungs, "Just get the freaking tacos!"* My daughter and I just kept looking at each other and I was about to go berserk. She has a little more patience with him than I do, but I could tell he was treading on thin ice with her. But being the patient daughter that she is with her *"older than dirt Daddy,"* she continued to humor him, and I had given up. He really isn't older than dirt; he just thinks he is when it suits him. And I call him that when it suits me!

The waiter came back again, we got beverage refills, another bowl of salsa, and I think that my husband was almost ready to order. So he told the waiter to get our order first, and then get back to him.

"Chicken fajita quesadillas, please," we almost said in unison. Done, we were done. And he was still looking at that dang menu. Even stuck a chip back in the salsa bowl and still hadn't given him an order. Boy, do those Mexican waiters have the patience of Job!

Finally, my husband placed his order. "Three tacos please!"

Thank the Lord *in Heaven and there is a God!* We weren't going to have to watch this poor waiter go to trial and prison for choking the life out of my husband. He was free at last! I bet he was saying, "Finally got that white man's order, and it only took ½ hour tops, and it was only three little tacos." I would have been embarrassed by all the delay and trouble to only order that much. But I ain't going there, I ain't, I ain't! I'll just leave the man alone with his tacos and dare his fork to come my way!

So we ate our dinner in peace, I asked my husband how he liked his tacos since he had put everything in God's sweet name on it. Then he said, "What's the name of those sauces over there?"

"Hon you don't want that, it'll burn you up!"

He was referring to three different strengths of hot sauces, which were in a container to my left.

"Hand me that little one."

"Those are just like Texas Pete, and if you want your mouth to catch on fire, you better lighten up!"

"Kelli, hand me that sauce."

She handed it to him, and he proceeded to shake it all over his tacos. Sprinkle, sprinkle, and pour! Better get out the fire extinguisher.

Since I had almost finished my meal, I proceeded to watch him eat those *"light your fire"* tacos that he just couldn't make his mind up that he wanted. I wouldn't be surprised if he had finished them and then asked to see the menu again for something else to eat. Well, bless my soul, he did eat every one of them, and when I asked him how they were he just said, "They're all right!" Just like that. So I thought to myself, *If they were just all right, I hate to see if he really liked them.* He would have picked the plate up and licked it clean, just like our dog Megan, except she would not have liked the hot sauce.

Finally we were finished, plates almost clean, except for the rice fillers that they give too much of. That poor defenseless waiter brought the check to our table and he asked if we needed anything else. Well, my son did not grace us with his presence, so my husband had to order him a *"to go"* burrito. He had to open the menu again, *God forbid*, and try to find "burrito" on the menu.

"Large or small, chicken or steak, with side or no side," too many decisions for my husband, so he looked at my daughter and me. I just looked down at the floor and pretended that I did not hear him. Kelli proceeded to tell the waiter what type of burrito we wanted, and my husband chimed in. "Maybe he wants a quesadilla, but what is that? Does it have beans in it? What kind of meat?" And I thought to myself, *"nobody cares what's in the freaking burrito, 'cause we're not going to be the one to eat it. Just get something before I strangle you and have to share a jail cell with this waiter."*

I felt myself slowly starting to slide under the table to the *pits of hell*, and I was going to take my husband with me. That poor waiter really was going to jail when he got through with my husband. And I could envision him reaching for a pistol in his pocket, no, a bazooka by this time.

Finally my husband, with my daughter's patience and urging, found something that was perfect to take home for my son: a chicken burrito, large, no sides. I had already slid underneath the table, and was going to try to get through the window to go home, but no such luck. The waiter left, and I bet he was thinking he was going to contaminate the heck out of that food order so that at least one of us would get sick and never come back here again. Probably didn't happen, but I bet he was thinking about it!

I was so ready to go, so our *"to go"* order took only about five minutes to get back to the table. And I could see the desperation in the waiter's eyes.

"Get out!" he seemed to be saying!

"Gotcha back, Jose!" (And his name was Jose, 'cause it was on his nametag, Welcome to Jose's!)

We got up, moved out of that booth, and made our way to the door and out. Finally; a sigh of relief from me and an echoing applause coming from inside the restaurant. *Ah … probably not for us!*

So the moral to this story is, don't take your husband to a restaurant that he says he doesn't like but shows up anyway. He's a man, you know, and they never can make up their mind! *Beg to differ?* And never give him a menu of food that he doesn't like; just order for him. Get plain food and hide the hot sauce, 'cause you'll be paying for it later! And for the sake of good Southern manners, I will not go into detail, but if you see me and pull me aside, I'll tell you.

And that's an end to this story that I can't bring myself to write, but I bet you can figure it out, but good luck on the next *"don't like it"* restaurant! Or you can just lie to your husband and tell him you're going to serve food at a homeless shelter, but with your luck he'd show up there too!

POLITICS, SPORTS
and the SCHOOL SYSTEM
... GIVE ME A SET *of* EARPLUGS!

I bet you're wondering why I wrote that! Well, I have a perfectly good answer, but it might be kinda mean to some of my relatives, most of all the one that I live with. But it's the dang truth, and I am going to tell you this little story, and then you can beg to differ. *But I bet you won't!*

For starters, we'll talk about the school system. I respect it, am 100% in favor of making it the best it can be for our children, and think the principals, teachers, and anyone else that is involved in the workload that it takes should be highly commended. I think it takes a special person to be involved in education, and they should be very proud of their accomplishments. And I am in no way, shape, form, or fashion poking fun at the school system itself, only for being the main topic, if not the *only* topic, when my husband and I are in the company of other educators.

When I married my fine channel-flipping husband, he was involved in the school system, and the twenty-three years that I have known him since, he is still involved in more than one way. He has been on the school board, school evaluator, assistant principal, director, athletic director, coach, county director, volunteer, principal, mentor, and I'm sure there is more but it is Friday, and I can't think very well right now. In a nut shell, or *a shotgun shell*, he has been involved in the school system or something with it his whole career.

He knows the school system inside and out and has played a lot of roles. He can tell you who, when, and what for and then some. He knows everybody and everything and can talk about it till the cows might decide to come home. In my case, the cows never come home, 'cause he *never* stops talking about it. He must have radar or something, since he can always finds someone to talk to about it.

You see, my husband comes from a long line of educators. His sister and brother are and were very active and highly respected in our community and around the state. They know a lot of people, have a lot of connections, and have statewide friends to talk with about the school system forever and ever amen. So if I want to get away from this conversation, *I don't have a prayer.*

I highly respect our school officials, teachers, etc., and I think they deserve all the praise that they are given. LORD knows I had trouble keeping my own kids' straight, and I know that there is no way in heck that I could have managed a whole room full of them or an entire building. Patience of Job, I say, and that I did not inherit from anyone since I am an *"instant gratification girl."*

I have been a nurse for three decades, but one thing that I do not do is *talk shop* at home. I guess I could come home and tell my family about all the gory things that happen at the hospital, all the infections that we deal with, and all of the wonderful odors that I get to whiff on a daily basis. *And it ain't the smells of Christmas!* Better yet, I could wait until we all sit down to dinner and really tell them how my day went, and see them one by one take their plate to the den. *Now ain't that mean!* (But payback is precious!)

But if you are out with your husband and his comrades, you are locked in: hook, line, and sinker. You have no place to go to escape this conversation, unless you want to go to the bathroom for a long siesta, take a phone call to a dial tone, or make wonderful friends with the bartender or the valet parking attendant, or learn to smoke. And after a while, my husband and his comrades will come and find you, and think that you are really strange, or rather much stranger than they thought you were. *I know this, 'cause I have tried.* I'm not strange, and by this time don't give *a rat's behind*, 'cause I'm just tired of hearing a conversation in which I am not involved in personally but by marriage only.

When you're a little bit ADD, my definition only for myself and this circumstance is, *"Attention Dunno Deficit,"* it's almost impossible to sit still and listen to a conversation when you don't have a clue what they're talking about. I fidget, mess with my hands, jewelry, cross and uncross my legs, shift in my seat, reapply my lipstick, drink a sip of something, then another sip until the glass is empty, and I'm throwing my hands up for a refill, looking around the room, eavesdropping on other people's conversations, etc. I also notice anyone else that is sitting at the table with *"deer in the headlights"* look on their faces, make eye contact, and telepathically say, "Wanna go smoke?"

While this is going on, mind you, my husband and his comrades have not missed a beat and have no clue that any other activity is going on at the table. *"Lost in Space,"* I call it, and it will take a while before they come back to the earth's atmosphere. Smoking sounds better all the time.

Since we cleared that topic up, let's move to the sports arena. I knew this too, way before matrimony was ever entered into the picture. Should have had a big clue when I found out he was a sports announcer every Friday night at our home football games and that he had just bought a sixty inch widescreen television. Certainly wasn't for his distance vision or the family channels.

Most of our dates, as I recall, centered around watching sports on television, going to college and high school football games, listening to them on the radio, going to Little League games, etc. This should have clued me in that this guy was a sports fanatic, but love blinded this, and I thought it was a passing phase. Wrong, wrong, wrong! So wrong!

When I met all of his family for the first time, I noticed that after dinner everybody would literally herd themselves to the den, find a comfortable spot, and glue themselves to the television. This was usually the *"belly up nap time"* that I was talking about, and most of them were asleep within the first hour. *And guess what was on the television?* You guessed it … a football, baseball, or basketball game. *Yeah!* And I was there to witness, participate, and stay for the whole ordeal, unless I managed to excuse myself, grab the car keys, and have to go out for *"necessities."* Necessities meaning ice cream, shopping, or doing anything to get me out of the house until the ball games were over.

I have to defend myself a little bit here as to the reason that I don't like to watch sports on television. You see, when I was growing up, no one in my family ever played sports, and my Daddy never watched it on television. So it is something that I just was not accustomed to, and didn't know a *blessed* thing about! It also did not excite me one "I-O-D-A," and it seemed to be the very lifeblood of my husband and his relatives.

Not that there is anything wrong with liking sports, but if I can find a good sale somewhere, I am *"poof be gone"* and it's heck with what ever sports event is on television. And that happens quite often.

My channel-flipping husband, and now my son, love sports, and this phase has never left either one of them. I have seen my husband have three televisions going at one time, a radio, and his headphones on, because he was afraid he was going to miss something. *And so what if he does?* The sun will still rise, and the world isn't coming to an end. But I have quit trying to tell my husband that, 'cause I lose every time, and he will argue with me until those cows do come home. And we're still arguing!

He gets on the phone with people, and they have to recite scores on every game that they have seen and argue about a point or two. *Who cares?* I guess they do! Why can't they just say so and so won the game or so and so lost the game? No, they argue about scores, plays, coaches, conduct, you name it, and will talk about it for weeks if it is a so-called *big game*. He acts like he was out there throwing the ball. I know I am not in his loop, and I am a female, but why is all this *horse hockey* so important and take up so much of their life? Must be a testosterone thing!

I think he would have to *"rock, paper, scissors"* with me to get him to miss a sports event, ah heck, you can forget it. This past New Year's Eve he didn't go to a party with me because the hostess didn't want to turn on the football game. And you couldn't blame her. *So guess what?* I went alone, and left his little sports fanatic self at home. I wasn't mad or nothing, just thought of it as a little stumbling block. *Boy, did he miss a good party!* Glad it wasn't my funeral. He really would have had a big decision to make.

Oh well, enough of that! You get the picture. So let's move on to politics. This might be the final blow, so listen up.

I am not a politics expert either. You might say I am well below a rookie. Oh, I watch television, I see the candidates or the chosen ones, I listen to their speeches, and I hear all the promises that they plan on keeping. All of them have something pretty to say, just the right things and not to offend anyone except for their opponent. I call it *romancing the public*. Just like another species that we know, that says all the right things so they can make the right moves. *Got it!*

Then I hear the other side, that all politicians are crooked, don't mean what they say, aren't going to do half of what they say, and then I'm supposed to choose a candidate based on what? Heck, then I'll just go for the candidate that has the best taste in clothes, maybe the best color palette. *Why?* Because this has to be a good sound choice because you will never hear the end of it if you make a bad choice of shoes more than a bad choice of words. *Am I right?* You better believe it!

Well, getting back to the political *thang*, my husband, his family and comrades, know how to talk this in the ground too! Hours and hours will go by, and they are still talking about it or fighting. One of our comrades, who will remain nameless, strikes up a political conversation every time we get together with them. When I hear the initial, "Did ya'll see so and so, that Democrat on the television…?" I want to kick my husband under the table so I can distract him. I am not ready for a *"rooster"* party tonight, and it happens every time. (A rooster party is when men try to outdo each other about everything!) *You know, the usual!*

My husband does love politics, and he gets so flustered about it that I swear he should run for office. I tell him that a lot, and he just says *no!* When he says that, I just say, "Well, you could wear all the designer suits and shoes, and get a fancy haircut, gotta look nice." Just look on the television and see how nice Barack and Hillary look; I wonder who does their hair? Her suit is nice, but she could up the pumps a little or a tad more jewelry wouldn't hurt. Look, Barack's teeth are so white they match his shirt. Probably uses those new whitening strips or has a new Sonic toothbrush.

My husband just looks at me and says, "You don't know a dern thing about politics, do you?" I just look at him with my sweet Southernism, and say, "I sure do, 'cause I've been listenin' to you for how many decades? I've listened to you so much or tuned you out, that I should be a dang expert! I'm also one in sports and in the school system. So if you want to fight about it, better get in line with your other friends and relatives. *'Cause I've been listenin' to them too!"*

Well, I haven't bought any earplugs yet, but I am fixin' to go get me a pair with a matching neck chain and start a fashion statement for all of us gals that have to listen to a whole lot but don't really want to. I wonder if that neck chain comes in sterling silver or shiny gold or in a color of choice?

Gotta be fashionable, ya'll, and we don't have to listen to anything that we don't want to! That's the Southern belle way, and don't you forget it! Or…at least it's my own sassy way, and I'm proud of it.

WHO PUT *the* EMPTY MILK CARTON BACK IN *the* REFRIGERATOR?

This is the story of my life! Empty milk cartons, empty juice cartons, empty cereal boxes, empty bread bags, and they always get put where they don't belong. And that is not where they came from like the refrigerator, the cupboard, or the breadbasket. Every time I reach for something and find an empty container without a dang thing in it, I want to yell at the top of my lungs, and it won't be *church* language.

The people that I live with, and they will remain nameless, most of the time put things in the trash when they are empty or at least leave them on the counter for me to pick up. But one of my family members who is about six feet tall and about twenty years old, is notorious for taking the last swig of milk, the last bit of juice, the last of the cereal, or the last piece of bread and putting the container right back where he got it. It's not that he is not intelligent, rather he is just lazy as all heck! *And I mean this with love!*

Every time I find his evidence in my fridge or cabinets, I scream and say, "Who put that empty milk carton back in the 'frigerator?" *Silence!* No response by anyone in the household. They just pretend they don't hear me, and I know they do. Even the dog and cat hear me because they run and hide. Everybody but the dang guilty parties!

Now, it might be just a little thing to most people to find an empty container in their kitchen, and they just throw it away. Don't make a fuss, don't say anything, just lovingly put it in the trash. *But dang it, I ain't gonna, without making some noise.* And a lot of noise I do make, like slamming doors, stomping my feet around, turning up the television, or just plain hollerin'.

If you think about it, and I'll do the math, we buy about two gallons of milk a week times fifty-two equals 104! The same with bread, 104. Juice is fifty-two at one carton per week. And cereal is two boxes per week, and that is also 104. So if I add it up, that will make about 364 times per year that I have to throw something away because somebody else forgot, or in my son's case, was just plain lazy. Don't you think this is excessive? That's more than every day of the year that I have to throw something away. *And I'm blasted mad that I have to do it too!* In other words, I am sick and tired of being sick and tired!

That's another thing about my family, they failed "Empty Container Disposal 101" aka ECD 101. *Failed miserably!* Took the course, didn't believe a word of it, failed the course, and got kicked out of my class. I guess they figure if Momma's in the house, then she'll take care of things like she always does, and having been doing it since they were born, or the older one, when we got married. My first mistake, my very big mistake!

Basically, my family is spoiled to the core! And I

made them that way, until just recently. I guess my momma spoiled me, and my Nanny spoiled her. *Dang it!* Look what has happened in a chain reaction. We have become lazy and uneducated individuals and can't pass ECD 101. I have allowed my family to assume this behavior and haven't done a dern thing about it until recently when I have begun expressing myself. *Loudly!*

I got on my so-called soap box last week and told them all how well they had it and that I was sick and tired of doing everything around here, and I didn't appreciate having to pick up after all of them. *Silence again!* Heads did hang a little bit. Silence continued. So I just said my peace again and asked them to help a little bit more around the house. And the first rule, and only rule that ticks me off at this time, is to put the dang empty containers in the trash.

Well, after my lecture things got a little bit better around the house, and I wasn't having to do as much! Containers were still left on the counter, but I seldom found one in the cabinet or refrigerator that was empty. I began to think that my tales of the soapbox had finally done some good. *At least for the meantime!*

Then little by little, containers started to appear empty again and left in off limits places. My voice, which had been reduced to normal, started to escalate again, and then to start yelling when I would find one of them. Instead of silence after my yelling now, it became the fading footsteps of my family leaving the house rather quickly and not taking the dang containers with them.

I guess I shouldn't fret about such things, little things like empty milk cartons and such. I should be thankful that I have a wonderful family and should learn to pick my battles. *Yes, I should!* But the more I think about it, the more I want to swat all of them up side the head with that empty milk carton, potato chip bag, cereal box, or whatever else I find that is empty! Wouldn't make them feel very good, but I would be so elated as a sly grin comes over my face. *And maybe they would get the hint?*

So this morning I got up at 3:55 am, since my rapid eye movement sleep no longer existed, perked a whole pot of coffee, took the dog out, and went and got the paper. No body else *up*, thank goodness, total quiet for me. I decided to read for a while, enjoy the solitude and contemplate my day. Picked up the laptop and was writing the last of this story. Really didn't have a good ending to it, or one that would satisfy me, so my brain felt like it is working pretty well this morning for only 3–4 hours of sleep.

After I fixed my cup of coffee, I went into the refrigerator, and guess what I saw? Guess! And guess again! It was an almost empty milk carton with just a tablespoon of milk in it. *Bless their hearts!* I bet they did that on purpose so they didn't tick momma off! *Guess again!* They wanted me to see it so I would get mad a little, pour it out, put it on the counter, and wait for myself to take it to the trashcan.

I am contemplating whether I will or not. Maybe I'll just leave it there, buy another carton, and pretend it's not there. Want to see how long it takes my lazy family to take it out of the refrigerator? Or I could be in for a long wait, like I usually do, and it ain't gonna happen. *Wanna make a bet on it?*

Or I could really tick my family off and wake them

up with a loud surprise this morning, scream loudly and ask as to who left an almost empty milk carton in the 'fridge, turn on all the lights, turn the music or the television up loud (and the dog howls when I do this), and stand back and watch the fireworks begin. *It's just 5am now you know!* I'm up, and I may as well feel the love and have the rest of the family up with me.

I might even have the last swig of milk in the jug, the end piece of bread for toast in the bread bag, the last teaspoon of grape jam in the jar, the spatula scrapings of butter in the butter bowl which contains some of the grape jam remnants, and have myself a little breakfast. Think I'll leave the empty containers all over the kitchen, including the twist tie from the bread bag (hate that too!), crumbs on the counter with sticky jam and butter, and leave. Yes I will, and the more I think about I'm laughing hysterically and give myself a high five. *My inconsiderate family won't know what hit 'em!* And I'm going to hide all the dishrags and cleaning stuff so they'll have to actually look for something to clean it up with. And the trashcan is going outside so they will have to look for it too! *Revenge is so sweet!*

MIDDLE AGE
and MOTORCYCLES

When I was about forty-five years of age, I was given a challenge: "Want to learn how to ride a motorcycle?"

And I said, "What the heck?"

You see, I live in a very motorcycle popular area, Myrtle Beach. Just about as many women ride solo as men. We have an annual fall and spring motorcycle rally, plus the Atlantic Beach Bike fest. We have other small rallies throughout the year, poker runs, you name it. A lot of locals and non-locals ride up and down Highway 17 whenever the weather is above fifty degrees. You see, on a bike, the temperature is around fifteen degrees cooler, but that doesn't stop them.

Getting back to my challenge, I sort of shrugged it off. *Me riding a motorcycle?* It will never happen. Well, I continued to think about it, and the more I thought about it, the more I liked the idea. I had always found bikes to be fascinating, loud, and a little bit rebellious. I fit some of those descriptions too, so I thought I might like to give it a try.

So I called up my channel-flipping husband at

work one day and said, "Do you mind if I learn to ride a motorcycle?"

His reply was, "Are you insane?"

"I guess!"

Why did I think to reason that he would answer me any other way? Besides, the most dangerous thing that I had ever done was riding a bicycle without a helmet and get on one of those roller coasters at the fair. And a Southern lady just didn't think to do things such as that. Don't want to mess up that *"do"*! Or have your brains scattered all over the sidewalk. *Shut my mouth!*

Well, after I gave this some thought and I do actually think sometimes, this Southern gal decided that she did want to do it, so I signed up for a beginner motorcycle course at the local technical college. *And guess what*? So did about thirty other middle-aged women. We had only three men in the class. Funniest dang thing I ever saw. The instructor was a big ole biker chick with a buzz cut. *Works for me!* She knew what she was talking about and had the clothes, boots, and the bike to prove it.

The lecture part of the class went very smoothly. I was in the game and learning a lot. I had read a complete beginners book (*Motorcycles for Dummies*) before I came to class, so I thought I was prepared. Little did I know that this was the easy part and the hardest part was yet to come.

In this class, we had little glorified mini bikes to learn how to properly ride. Mini bikes, my butt, they were high-powered monsters that didn't give me a break for two days. I was scared to death the first time I just got on one of these little monsters, and even more scared when I had to crank it up. But the instructors took it slowly, Buzz and the gang, and I slowly progressed in the class. Back and forth, back and forth, in first gear, until we had mastered the little monster. At least that part!

We kept back and forthing it for a few hours, then we shifted into 2nd gear, and this let us do a little more. We went around cones, turned corners, and got to practice for Buzz. I couldn't hear for all the noise, so half the time I couldn't hear what Buzz was saying. What the heck, I just made up my own program. She kept saying, "Didn't you hear me?" And she would wave her arms, and I would nod and kept on doing my own program. I hate to perform like a pony for a crowd anyway, so I didn't do too well by Buzz's standards. I wanted to tell her to *"kiss my assets,"* but I finished the class and told her on the way out that I would be back there again for the intermediate class.

After the class, a month passed and I had not done anything more with my newly acquired skills. Not until the next bike week rolled around. I was sitting at the top of the hill in my neighborhood with my channel-flipping husband, who was not flipping at the time, watching the motorcycles go by, and the bug hit me. *I had to have a motorcycle!*

Well, bless my britches, a girl at work was selling her new red Honda, and I went to look at it. She was gorgeous: bright, shiny, and clean as a whistle! But...since I was such a bad student, I took a fellow biker friend with me to try her out. She ran smoothly, had enough power for me, so I decided to buy it. Without ever cranking it up or riding it by myself, I let my biker friend make the decision for me. I signed the check and away we went! Or rather, I let my friend ride it away.

I was now the proud owner of a new red Honda motorcycle that I couldn't even ride! *Well, what do I do now?* My friend made it easy for me, so she told me to get on it, I started it up, and put it into first gear. Slowly but surely the bike engaged and started down the road. I had begun! Down the rode I went, with my friend behind me, and I was riding. Made a half circle, turned right, then another half circle, and the bike was still up, and my butt was not on the ground. My friend motioned for me to stop; I turned the bike off and waited for some very serious criticism. Nope, she said, "You are riding so well!" Well what the heck, I had done it, and I was doing it. I think I did it just to spite Buzz!

After this, I was on my way! Riding faster and faster, I became more confident each day and became a pretty good biker. *Who says that middle age has to slow anyone down?* (I would like to meet that person and smack 'em!) I had accepted a challenge, taken it, and overcome the thought that another middle-ager didn't think I could do it. All I needed was a little confidence! Well bless my soul; I began to love riding a motorcycle!

I liked and do like to ride up and down Highway 17 with the rest of the beach traffic. I like to ride on the beachfront roads and look at the ocean and the marsh. I don't ride in freezing weather though, has to be about 70 plus degrees. Things just look different on a bike, and the freedom is great. I relax, think a lot about things, and it's something I can do that not a lot of people can.

Riding a motorcycle is therapy for me. You can think about more things and clear your head when you're on a bike. I used to think that bikers were a little *"way out there,"* so to speak, but now I'm glad I'm way out there too with the rest of them. Bikers are a different breed and rightfully so. They aren't so consumed by what other people think, they are truly individualists and find a lot of pleasure in what they do. Good for them and good for me!

So Southern girl, if you want to go out and learn to ride a motorcycle, and you're middle-aged like me, don't let anyone stop you! Because honey, you don't live but once, so live it like you want to. *Bless your heart and happy riding!*

And if you happen to go to that technical college and want to make a certain person's day, tell Buzz I said hello, and I just might be coming back to make her day!

MENOPAUSE
and MAYBE ME

Just let me tell you up front and center, that meno-pause is the pits! It will sound like the pits until I get to the end of this story. Middle age is not so bad, it's even quite good, but this *"thing"* that I mentioned is beyond explanation. Whoever said that this phase of a woman's life is not so bad *must be a man*!

This menopause stage of my life started in my mid/ late forties, so I can probably thank my lucky stars for that! Some women I know start much earlier and have to wait it out a whole lot longer. A little surgical inter-vention that I had in my thirties took away some of the landmarks to measure this great phase of my life. But the doctor left just enough of what female parts that I did have to still have those flashes of warmth that most women hate.

What is menopause anyway? And why do we call it that? You notice it has "men" in it, and it doesn't have a dang thing to do with them or does it? By the end of this story though, there might be an explanation as to why "men" are in this equation.

My first symptoms were just little light warmth flashes that I hardly even noticed. *Ha!*, I thought to myself, *if this is it, then what's all the fuss about?* Well, these little hot flashes got bigger and bigger, and pretty soon they were more than a flash, but a lightning bolt. I remember when I went on a cruise last year that these bolts were occurring about every thirty minutes. *And I was relaxing!* What was going to happen if I were really stressed? I shot so many bolts that Zeus didn't have anything on me!

Another thing about this wonderful time in your life is the fact that you probably need medication to stay sane. Well, I was never the one to take medicine, so I wanted to try something natural. I tried soymilk; couldn't stand the taste of the stuff. I tried black cohosh; made me tired but the warmth still prevailed. I tried cold showers, opening the windows in winter and freezing everyone in my household, limiting the amount of caffeine that I drank and bit the head off of everyone that came near me, rode a bike and exercised until I was soaking wet, not much different than a night sweat. Finally, I gave up. I needed *drugs!*

It's not so easy finding a solution for a menopause drug. First you have to have a reliable doctor, and one that knows what the heck they are doing. Your best bet is a female. How in the devil can a male doctor tell you what you can expect from these drugs when he's never experienced *"the curse"* or taken the drugs himself? When you get to this point in your life, you don't have time to mess around. *Halleluiah and amen to that!*

Bless my sweet doctor's heart! She isn't Southern by birth, but a transplant, and she is one of the cutest women I know! And has the most patience. No wonder it takes a month or two to get an appointment, and she takes about forty-five minutes with you when you get there. Women are probably hard to decipher, even though she is one, and I am no exception. I do get my money's worth when I see her and tell her every ailment I have. LORD knows when I'm going to get my foot back in the door, and I don't want her to miss nothing!

She started me on one medication, but it didn't decrease my lightning bolts or improve my mood any. Just ask my family! So we went from plan A, to plan B, then plan C, and finally we came up with a combo package that would do the trick. You know, after all this, I understand why some women think things are hopeless. But, I guess I was lucky, 'cause it only took about five different tries to get it right or to make it tolerable. But, I didn't say the *party* was over yet!

Menopause causes you not to be as affectionate as you were in your younger years. And after a twenty-three year relationship, who cares? You know your spouse inside and out just about as well as you know yourself, so this stage in your life is really not a good measure of your affectionate nature. Also, if you're lucky enough to have kids, they are almost or are grown, and you'd just as well give them a slap on the butt as a kiss on the cheek; also not a good measure. When you become middle-aged, you probably have seen, heard, and experienced enough to say that every little bit of excitement that comes along, doesn't cause you to jump up and down anymore.

People also talk about your energy level during this trying time. Heck, I probably have more of it. With no kids in tow, not wanting to cook or clean like I used to (I used to disinfect everything), going to where I want and when I want, I think my energy level is probably much better. Now I'm not too tired to exercise, it's actually kinda fun, and find that I don't put the demands on myself that I did when I was younger. *'Cause who the heck cares anyway?*

As for some people that say you probably don't feel as much like a woman, well, they can just *shut their mouths*! I think I feel more like one since I am really my own woman now, and not somebody else's picture of one. Middle age and especially menopause makes you saucy and sassy. You tend to speak your mind a lot more, 'cause you can, and you don't care what other people think anyway. Shouldn't have cared your whole life, but you grew up and were taught different. Heck, I started telling my kids to be their own person when they were little, and I still believe that. You can still be Southern and have manners, but you don't have to inhale everyone else's opinion. *Whew ... that was a mouth full!*

Well, since I started writing this, I realize that my experience with menopause ain't so bad! I feel like I am lucky enough to have gotten to live to this point in my life, count my blessings that I have a wonderful family that understands me and tolerates me without locking me out of the house, and enough money that I can go shopping and buy those tacky clothes that all you non-menopausers talk about. (I don't think that is even a word.) But I haven't bought anything purple yet, just bright pink and red, so I'm still safe. But if I buy purple tomorrow, it will mean that I have just reached another stage in my life, and I'll try to tackle whatever it has to dish out!

You see, I'm a Southern woman through and through,

and one of the most stubborn that you will ever find, except for my Nanny! I usually will not let anything get the best of me, especially when other people say it will. I love a challenge! And this is a dang good one.

And did we find out why menopause has "men" in it? I bet we could take a very big guess, and it won't be pretty!

So to all of my women friends, just hang in there, take your medicine and go buy something. Shoot, hasn't been a challenge yet for me that a little perfume, silk, or diamonds can't fix or at least make it tolerable. *Mmm*...I may need to go get my pocketbook! Or my husband's credit card; now where is it?

WHOSE TURN IS IT TO TAKE *the* DOG OUT?

Kids or children are a blessing, and we do tend to spoil them when they are growing up. We give them presents for every holiday, birthday, Christmas or Hanukkah, accomplishment, etc. *We do give them too dang much!*

When we decided to move from our last residence to Myrtle Beach, South Carolina, we didn't tell our youngest child until we were two weeks from moving. Wanting to soften the blow of creating a major stressor in his middle school life, we told him we were moving, and then that we were going to get him a dog, all in one breath. I don't think my son could decide whether he wanted to cry because we were moving or to scream for joy at finally getting the beagle that he had been begging for.

Josh, my son, had mentioned to me several weeks before that he wanted to get a beagle.

"Why in the heck do you want a beagle?" I asked.

"Because I want a boy's dog, not that sissy Shih Tzu that we already have!"

He explained to me that he wanted a dog that he could play with and teach tricks to. Our other dog just lay around all the time, and the only trick she could do was to lick herself. *Ain't that mean!*

At the time I had said no, but the more I thought about it, the more the idea appealed to me. This could help him to adjust to the move and give him something to focus his attention on. Also, it was kinda like giving him a $100 bill and saying, "Go spend it!" We wanted to soften the blow as much as possible, so we decided to cave in.

At first, I wasn't too keen on a beagle. We had a couple while I was growing up, but they were nothing special. My neighbors had them when I was growing up in the *"sticks,"* but they were always in outdoor pens, and no one paid them much attention. They were hunting dogs and were loaded on the back of a truck every Saturday to go and catch rabbits.

I looked in the paper one day and saw a breeder in Appling, Georgia, and gave him a call. We decided to drive out that day just to see the beagle puppies, but I knew that was not going to be the case. There were eleven of them in a pen and all males from the same litter. They all looked identical. They were tricolored beagles, and I picked the smallest one. He was a cantankerous little puppy, and I picked him up right away and knew I had to take him home. This story has already moved from Josh's dog to "my" puppy. I decided to name him Boomer after Josh agreed, and we took "my" puppy home!

Boomer was the cutest thing you ever saw, and I couldn't get enough of him. I played with him from morning till night. He was adorable! I left him with Josh and his sister Kelli every day and had to call every few hours to check on my new *child*.

"Did you take the puppy out, what is he doing, did you clean up after him!" I couldn't wait to get home to him in the afternoon so we could continue our bonding.

Kids tend to promise when you get them something like a new pet that they are going to clean up after it, feed it, and take it out to potty! Slowly but surely I saw these behaviors disappear from my son's daily regime, and soon became more of mine. I rapidly became the one to take the dog out in the morning, after work, after supper, and at bedtime. I was also the one to make sure he had food in his bowl and water in the other. I was also the one that went around the yard with a *poop bag* in my hand and cleaned up after him. I don't remember my son ever volunteering for that chore, or anyone else in the household (I may be exaggerating a bit here!) unless I shamed them into it.

As Boomer grew up, he seemed to look to me for everything. I also think I was the only one in the household that tended to his every need. I was the one that put a fan in his pen when it got hot, gave him a bath outside with the hose pipe, or put him in my marble tub when it got too cold, gave him his medicine, took him to the vet, took him for golf cart rides, for long walks, cut his nails after I bargained with him for a dog biscuit, and gave him so many pieces of ice that his teeth chattered. I guess by this time I didn't mind taking the dog out.

Josh did teach him a few tricks; how to sit, roll over, scratch your belly, and shake hands. We also taught him to do things on command if he wanted a cookie. Josh and I did have to bargain as to whom was going to take him out, and even got my husband involved.

No, channel-flipping husband was already involved from the beginning. So, Josh only had to take him out about 1/3 of the time, which wasn't in the deal, and this fraction slowly but surely progressed from one quarter to one tenth of the time. Boomer drank a lot of water and had to go often, and when he gave you *"the look,"* you better make it snappy!

"Ah Mom," was what I heard a lot from Josh!

"Don't ah Mom me, just get off your butt and go take the dog out!"

He would slowly rise, shuffle his feet a bit, give out one of those teenage snorts, and sachet down the hall.

"Come on, Boomer! I just took you out!" He would snap on the leash, pull Boomer out the door, and he would be back in less than five minutes. *Fastest pee-er in the South!* Funny how when I took him out, I would be out there for twenty minutes plus! Kids!

This went on for most of Josh's teenage years, and Boomer's, until he went away to college. Then I had to bargain with my channel-flipping husband to take him out. Usually I would get the answer, "I'll do it in a minute, or I'll do it on the next commercial," which used to drive me insane. Many times I have had to go and get the towel, because my husband couldn't miss a sports play. *Dang television!*

All in all, I was Boomer's mom, and he was my child. I probably treated him better than my children, because he didn't talk back or give me a hard time about anything. Just gave me unconditional love all the time, whether I was in a good mood or a bad one. But when he was around, I was usually in a good one.

After five years of taking this dog out several times a day and tending to his every need, this story ends on a sad note. When he was just over five, we found out that he had liver failure, and we lost him six months later. Devastation had hit our family, and it was several months before any of us wanted to look at another dog. But the time came for us, mainly me, to look again for a dog that I needed and one that really needed me.

I was lucky and felt that God had a hand in it, and I drove to Aiken, South Carolina, to adopt another beagle. Her name is Megan, and she has become one of the joys of my life and a constant companion. She has given to this family what Boomer's death had taken away.

Now, for me personally, it is not a chore for me to take the dog out, but I now consider it a blessing. Every moment that I can spend with her and do for her is not a chore, but something that I enjoy doing.

Now, we don't have to bargain, draw straws, or whatever to see who takes the dog out. No more yelling at my son or channel-flipping husband to do it! I cherish what I've been given and consider it a second chance.

Just remember, when the dog has to go out, just do it! Consider it a privilege to have a beloved pet, and it will also keep your momma from hollering and the floors and carpet will stay much drier!

Megan sends a nudge to all of you!

NO WHITE SHOES
AFTER LABOR DAY

id you ever hear your momma say that? "You can't wear white shoes after Labor Day; *it ain't allowed!*"

Momma wouldn't let us wear white shoes, white pants, white anything if it was after the last holiday before the fall hit. No use trying to sneak and do it, 'cause that woman had radar! And if she saw you in it, you might as well make an about face, and go change, 'cause you weren't going to leave the house like that!

In the late 70's, when I moved to South Florida, you know, *the Sunshine State*; we had a lot of sunshine and a lot of hot, very humid weather. Well, my parents came to visit, and I had on white pants. Momma looked me up and down when she saw me and said, "It's after Labor Day, and you're wearing white?"

I just grinned and said, "Yes ma'am, it's hotter than a blue blazes down here, and I'm wearing summer clothes. I realize its December, but that's what we do down here."

Momma and Daddy stayed with us for about a week, and she had a hard time wearing white shoes and white pants. I had the windows open, the fans going, and she was sitting on the bed perspiring.

"Can you turn the air conditioner on, I am just a sweating?"

"Sure, Momma, but don't try to wear one of those turtlenecks and boots that you brought, 'cause it won't help none!"

I did turn the air conditioner on, and she did finally put her fall clothes from home away. Actually took out some white pants, but I could tell that you was not comfortable wearing them.

Ain't it funny how so many traditions have been adopted through the years but seem so funny and downright silly after a while. Another funny tradition that got thrown out the window was not to go barefoot until after May 1st.

With today's global warming, I've seen people going barefoot at the beach until after December. They give a quick rest and start again the end of February or the first of March. Kids, rather teenagers, have bare feet with sandals on all winter long. *What the heck?* No wonder they are sick half the time, or at least that's what their forged illness excuse says! *Shut my mouth!*

When I was a kid, I would count the days until I could go barefoot or *barefooted* as my momma used to say. And I did have to wait until *the* day. One time my Aunt Linda said that she went barefoot several days before May 1st, and I was appalled. How dare she go against the rules, and my momma wouldn't let me? Not fair!

May 1st would come and off my socks and shoes would go. It was great to put your bare feet on the ground, but it was still a little cool. Rocks caused your feet to be more tender, so you walked a little slower and a little more crooked. *You remember?* Ants might bite your feet; you would step on a sticker and get a splinter in your foot. Going barefoot then might not be the most comfortable feeling in the world, but you had waited since Labor Day to do this! So you felt like you had to do it!

Going barefoot was just something that little Southern country kids did and did it all the time. Heck, I think most kids and teenagers did when I was growing up, that was the *"norm."* I don't remember wearing shoes much after May 1st thru Labor Day, except to church and when we had to go to school. It sure did feel funny to put your feet in those leather shoes or tennis shoes when you had to. Your feet and toes had been free most of the week, and now you had to cram them into those shoes, and most of the time had to wear socks too; little white anklets with lace or those plain white stretchy kinds. I really don't remember having any other color when I was a little kid.

We walked barefoot everywhere too! Out in the yard, on a hot sidewalk or street, on a rocky road, and didn't think a thing about it. Putting shoes or sandals on didn't cross my mind much. I still remember going on dates in high school, me and my boyfriend both barefoot, and that was just the norm. We would dress up a little, but our feet were always bare. When I tell people about it now, they can't stop laughing! And to tell you the truth, I couldn't understand what they were laughing at. *Didn't everybody do that?* Heck, times sure have changed.

Wearing pants to church was also something that wasn't done in my childhood or in my teenage and young adult years. *Oh my!* I always had to wear dresses, and mine were usually at my knees or just a hint above. Pants could be worn at home or on the weekends, but never to church. I couldn't even wear them to school until I was in middle school. *Boy, that wouldn't go today*! Pants are worn everywhere, and you don't see dresses much either. Shorts are more of the norm at the beach!

When I was around twelve, my momma made me a pants suit to go to a boy-girl party. It had a tunic top and bell bottom pants. It looked great at the time. But since I was not allowed to wear it to school or to church, it just hung in my closet for several months. I got invited to another party and just took it out of my closet without trying it on and put it in my suitcase. When I got to the party, I put the pants suit on, and it was way too short, and I was very embarrassed. I had the highest *"high water"* pants you have ever seen. Just had a growth spurt and didn't realize it!

Funny things like these probably don't happen anymore! We wear white all year long, depending on the weather and the circumstance. We also have our feet exposed a lot, and going barefoot is just second nature. Especially on the coast in the South, we don't think about it. Wearing pants is a norm; I really feel like I am dressing up to put on a dress. And the casual lifestyles of today don't have a lot of room for dressing up.

But these are memories of mine that my children will never get to experience, and like my momma and daddy before me, I'm sure they have memories that I will never be able to experience either. Memories are special, but they show us that the world is changing, sometimes for the better, sometimes not. I sorta like some of the old ways of doing things, so I try to preserve some of the traditions. I also listen to my elder kinfolks when they tell us things when they were when they were growing up. And it seems that my family is getting smaller by the years, so when I do get a chance to listen, I do!

So wear your white, go barefoot, and put your jeans on wherever and whenever you want to! Cause, honey child, every day is *"wear what you want day"* in my opinion, and a Southern girl always gets her way, at least most of the time!

DON'T BLOW YOUR NOSE AT *the* TABLE

If I had done this when I was growing up, my momma would have slapped me silly! Not really, but that is something that you just did not do at her dinner table, or breakfast or lunch table for that matter. Nose blowing was to be done in private, preferably away from everybody: the bathroom, your room or outside. *Never in the company of other people!* It was just plain rude, crude, and uncouth, and I heard this for most of my growing up life.

Most Southerners are raised or reared to have good manners; at least my generation was. Not to say that people in other parts of the country weren't raised or reared with good manners, but the South is just different in how we are taught. You can usually recognize a Southerner by the way in which they express their manners, that's all.

From the day a child is old enough to understand, Southern children are taught manners. "Thank you" or "ta ta" is one of the things that they are taught first, besides "Momma" and "Daddy." Then as they learn to understand, they are taught "please," "yes ma'am and no ma'am," "yes sir and no sir," "may I," "excuse me" to name a few.

It's like music to my ears when I hear a little child talk so politely at such a young age; it's a Southern tradition.

When I was growing up, I was taught some other things that were drilled into a little lady. I wasn't exactly a little lady, but a rowdy tomboy, but I had to act like a lady on certain occasions, especially when my momma gave me the evil eye, and she did that very well. She probably learned it from my Nanny.

I was taught not to talk loud in company. This was especially hard for me since I already had a loud indoor voice, and when I got excited, it got louder. You could always pick me out of a crowd, because I was so loud, louder than most kids. I was the one that got a C in conduct, but I just couldn't tone it down. I always wondered why some of my friends never got below an A in conduct and always talked so softly. Just not in my genes! *And it still ain't!*

My Nanny told me to always smooth my dress down before sitting down. Well, I could do that without any problem, since I always had to wear a dress. And when you don't shave your legs in 6th grade, you did wish that you were wearing pants. Nowadays, they shave them in 4th grade, but they get to wear pants. *That's beside the point*! When you stood up though, your dress was always wrinkled or waded up in the back, but I did smooth it down first.

I was also told to stand up straight or sit up straight on a daily basis. You would swear my momma had gone to a first-rate charm school. She always said she was going to send me to one. *I never did believe her though!*

She would come up behind me and push on my back and put her hands on my shoulders.

"You are going to be round shouldered if you don't stand up straight!" One time she put a book on my head and made me walk around with it. It did fall off a few times, but that was part of *the school*. At the dinner table or supper table, as we used to call it, she would make me sit up straight. I just wanted to eat and get up, but this was also part of the school too!

I managed to survive this era of my life, and then there were other mannerisms that I had to learn:

1) Don't talk with food in your mouth! *It looks like the inside of a washing machine.*

2) Chew your food slowly! *Don't eat so fast, you'll get indigestion.*

3) Girls don't call boys. *But I called them a lot of things, and some of them weren't nice.*

4) Sip, don't gulp! *The burp will come up faster.*

5) Introduce the older person first, then the younger. *Old man this is … …*

6) Let the boy open the door for you. *Then step on his foot on the way in.*

7) Offer your guests to sit down. *Wanna take a load off?*

8) Don't pick your nose! *At least not where anyone can see you.*

9) Don't stare at people directly! *A mirror works much better.*

10) Ladies don't burp in front of other people. *Wait until you're outa earshot!*

11) Make sure your slip doesn't show. *Nowadays, it's fashionable.*

12) Don't sass me! And don't talk back! *You know Momma is gonna git the last word.*

13) Sit up straight! *Look like you belong in the military.*

14) Don't slouch! *Ditto to the above.*

I could go on and on, but this is all that I can remember for now. Some of these I did teach my children, but a lot of them I did not. Probably because times are different, and I was too busy trying to keep up with them, and to keep them from misbehaving; you know, that "child abuse" thing that we were talking about! And I probably was sassing my momma in my mind when she used to preach to me, and that's exactly what I was thinking.

Maybe when I was growing up, drilling all this stuff into children probably made us the way we were. I think we did respect our elders, especially our parents, and we were afraid to talk back or disobey. Today kids sort of *"run the show"* at times and talk back, regardless of the consequences. You know that child abuse thing is a boundary, and a simple spanking might put you in jail, or at least the fear of it. Heck, if we knew we were going to get a spanking when we were growing up, that put the fear of God in us enough!

Spanking when we were growing up wasn't child abuse, in my opinion. Because our parents loved us, they needed to punish us, and just a "go to your room" didn't get it most of the time, especially if you had a television, record player, or stereo, a radio, and a telephone in there. Punishing to my parents included a swat on the behind, once maybe twice, and then I was sent to my room to think about it some more. But not before they had unplugged every blessed thing in my room and took the telephone out. After a while, when I had thought about it, I usually went out and apologized and was always given open arms and a neck to hug. Now, does that sound like a prison sentence or child abuse to you?

Oh well, we were taught some very valuable things by our momma and daddy, but probably just as much from our grandparents. Remember, they were our surrogate parents. My kids were taught some of these things, not as much, because their grandparents weren't around as often, certainly didn't raise them like mine did. And in the future, these things will be taught even less. It's a shame that some of our heritage seems to die a little bit with each generation.

But don't you never mind! I'll still correct my grown children when they stray form the old traditions and mannerisms and hope someday to teach my grandchildren. I do get the "Oh, Mom!" and the "What?" with a cross-eyed look, but I still prevail. Oh well, can't ever say that I let a good thing die intentionally, except maybe a houseplant!

FORGET *the* BAGELS *and* CREAM CHEESE, PASS *the* BISCUITS PUH...LEASE!

outhern people or rather people that like real *"soul"* food, know how to eat! At least we know how to eat the stuff that will really *stick to your ribs.* You wouldn't ever find a true backwoods Southerner that grew up in the sticks like me, eating a bagel and cream cheese when I was growing up. I would probably have asked you, "What the heck are you talking about?" But it probably would have been a lot more colorful.

As I mentioned, soul food is food that truly comforts the soul. It gives you a warm, comfortable feeling that comes from good ole home cookin'. You can't get the same feeling from a Big Mac and a large order of fries. The person that prepared it usually makes this comfort food with time, effort, pride, and love. It gives them a warm feeling to serve it and a warm feeling for the person that consumes it.

A true Southern breakfast at my house consisted of bacon, scrambled eggs, grits, sausage, toast, butter and jelly, and occasionally some pancakes with syrup. Momma would get up way before anyone else did, and have this on the table before your feet ever hit the floor. You would wake up to the smell of bacon and sausage frying. My Grandma did the same thing and got up before it was ever daylight, and you could smell the coffee, and it was Luzianne. *Boy, that would clean your pipes and wake you up!*

I wonder if anyone ever brews that stuff anymore? And it was always in a coffee pot on the stove or a percolator on the counter. Both of them were always stained to death and never were their original color. I used to like to watch the coffee brew in that glass top that was on the stove coffee pot. You never see those things anymore, except in an antique shop. It sure brings back memories.

My Nanny or my Grand Daddy Paul used to let me drink coffee when I was a little girl. I had one of these coffee cups, not a mug, and would put several sugar cubes in it, and several spoonfuls of Cremora in it. *Man, I liked that stuff!* I would stick my spoon in it and eat it like ice cream. The sugar cubes too! I never see those anymore either, but they sure were fun to eat!

I don't remember my momma or daddy ever letting me drink coffee, in fact, I know they didn't. They seldom let me drink soda, except the cheap kind (my parents were extremely thrifty). And I liked Pepsi! Maybe that was why I was a little wound up when I was at my grandparents' house. And that's because they let me drink or eat whatever I wanted, as I told you earlier: a little spoiled Southern belle.

Getting back to soul food, let's not forget a good ole Southern Sunday dinner meal. We would have fried chicken, country-style steak with gravy, butter beans with fat back, mashed potatoes, macaroni and cheese (not the box kind), collard greens and good ole homemade biscuits and butter. There was always plenty of sweet tea, not this unsweetened kind that you had to add sweetener to, and some type of cobbler for dessert, cake, or pie. Everything was always homemade, and it was a rarity to find any part of that meal that came out of a box!

But times and foods have changed. The population's weight has gone through the roof, cholesterol and triglycerides are bad, and Lane Bryant is making a fortune! Well, a little exaggeration here! The population as a whole is more health conscious and good ole Southern food everyday at every meal is far too much for most people to handle.

Nowadays, people, including Southerners, opt for Granola and yogurt for breakfast, salads and water for lunch, then a light meal at supper of lean meat, salad again, and fruit. Gone are the homemade biscuits, butter and jelly, fatback, and all the fried foods, at least on a daily basis; now maybe on a weekly or monthly basis.

I usually have biscuits now only on holidays that come once or twice a year. They have been replaced by bagels or muffins, usually the whole-wheat kind, and always hold the butter. Light margarine will have to do!

Pretty soon, our old Southern diets will be in a history book somewhere that our grandkids can drool over. Our grandmothers really knew how to cook Southern-style, and this is a dying art. Every food store you go into has readily prepared food, so there's no reason to cook anymore. They don't teach home economics in school like they used to, so kids have lost interest. Oh well, I hope somebody writes it down. And I'm writing as fast as I can!

So if you like Southern food, sit down and eat it like there's no tomorrow whenever you get a chance. Good food is like a good memory, and LORD knows we could use more of them. So if you see me sometime out eating a big plate of fried chicken with a piece of bread in my hand, you can be dang sure that it won't be a bagel!

Happy and good Southern eating, ya'll. Now pass the biscuits! But hold that light margarine please, and give me the real thing!

NOT ANOTHER FAMILY REUNION!

Don't get me wrong! I love to go and visit family members, even a whole herd of them, even a whole herd of them in the same house at the same time. I don't mind it at all! But ask me to go to a family reunion that might last for more than a day, well I might tell you that I'll pass!

No, I won't do that either, 'cause if I did I would get the evil eye from one of my prominent immediate family members that I just happen to share a room with. I would also get the "silent treatment" and the nasal snorting that you can hear everywhere in the house. Some lip-poking involvement might also be accounted for...so I'm tired of seeing the suffering and hearing the whining, so I guess I'll go!

But...it's not *my* family reunion. It's my family by marriage. And I don't know ever-blessed relative that my husband has. I don't think he really does either! That's what's funny! How can you talk to people you don't know for more than a day? Just isn't my idea of a good time!

Ain't no use in arguing, 'cause you ain't gonna win this battle. Two Southerners in a headlock over who is right? And if one of them is a stubborn male, forget it.

He just talks louder, that's all! You notice I didn't say anything about a stubborn female, but that's beside the point in this story.

Well, I took my little self to the reunion, and didn't even kick and scream. Or rather the family reunion caravan drove me: my husband, his sister, his brother, and our sister-in-law. Not a bad ride, since Lenora the sister-in-law and I chatted all the way there. We just wanted something good to eat and a drink if we could have gotten away with it.

When we finally arrived at the reunion house, I was surprised to see that it was in a beautiful old Southern, white-columned mansion/house that was in a little podunk town, about the size of nothing. Whew... it was really podunk, but cute if I might add. I don't think there was but one stoplight, and it might not have been a true stoplight, but just said *caution*. Ain't enough traffic out here!

The house was just as beautiful inside as I could imagine. It was filled with more antiques than most fine stores could hold. Immaculate furnishings, drapes, collectables, paintings, etc.; it had it all. I saw people coming and going out of that house like a beehive, and I really didn't know a blessed soul, at least not to start with.

Well, my husband obviously did, and took off the minute he entered the front porch to visit with his relatives. I was more interested in looking at the paintings and wallpaper than talking to people that I had never seen in my life. I decided to just look at the rest of the house and amuse myself for the next hour of the 24 hours that I would be here.

The house was incredible, definitely worth going

to the reunion for, and I couldn't believe that this little town could have a house this fine. It looked like something out of a movie. But after walking through this house and up the staircase, I found something awfully odd about it. It was as cold as an icebox! The owner obviously was very hot natured and had the thermostat turned down to fifty! *My gosh*, I thought, *how could anyone stand it this cold, and pay the power bill, to boot! Must be how they preserve the place.*

Well, after going and getting my sweater, I decided to glide around to the refreshment table, which was set up very elegantly in the fine dining room! I looked down to pick up what looked like a little pecan pie, and I could feel all eyes upon me! Maybe I wasn't supposed to eat those? Nah...I proceeded to pick it up, put it on a napkin, and took a bite. Eyes were still on me! *Maybe they don't think I'm a relative?* But how would they know? No one seemed to know anybody else! Or at least that was the impression that I got!

Pretty table, pretty flowers, and pretty cake; still didn't know any of these people! Everyone was standing around munching and crunching, drinking and blotting, shifting their feet, holding their pinkies up, but still no one acted like they knew anybody else. Oh well, I think I'll back track and look at the house some more!

I went back out into the hall, and glory be, I found someone that I knew. It was my husband's aunt. A sweet little gray-haired lady, cute as could be, and she was about 90 years old. She kept looking at me with those puzzled eyes, though. Maybe my makeup was on crooked, or my lipstick has smeared? No...she just didn't have the foggiest idea who I was. And when I told her who I was, she called me by the wrong name. *Don't you just love it, bless her heart.*

After freeing myself from her gaze, I slipped out to the kitchen area and found one of my husband's cousins. A very nice woman that actually knew my name, and to be honest, I hardly knew hers. We chatted for a while, and then she pulled out this silver medallion and started swinging and talking to it, asking it questions and such. Just didn't want her to ask it any personal questions about me, so I made a quick but polite exit. *Ain't no sense in being truthful at this point.*

I think then it was time for me to head to the spiked punch bowl, if there was such a thing. But I didn't see anything that resembled a *"naughty"* bowl of spiked punch, didn't really see any punch inside at all. Wonder if I can make some, if I can go back to the car and see if anyone brought their own *"comfort."*

I walked around looking lost and bumped into more and more relatives. Or rather they bumped into me; another sweet little aunt that actually knew my name. I gave her a hug and a kiss and then moseyed on to the next relative. A trio of cousins that all had the same mother, the same smiles, and the same way of greeting, "Hi, how ya dooin'!" A little gray haired man that struck up a conversation that lasted quite some time, and then come to find out, he wasn't even a relative. I don't even think he was at the right house.

"Birthday party? What birthday party?" I said.

And another man that came up and gave me a kiss, a wink, and I never did find out who he was. Men tend to do that to me though. Must be the Southern Belle *"act"!*

I found some more relatives and talked about their

kids, their accomplishments, how much money their kids were making, how they ranked on the social scale, how many kids their kids had, what sports the kids of their kids were playing, what colleges they went to, who they married (*don't have a clue*), where they were living, what their current jobs were if they had one, who they knew or associated with, and what political party they campaigned for. Just to throw it in, I wondered what their favorite bar was, where it was located, and how come they weren't there instead of here. Ha! Should *shut my mouth*, but I had to throw it in to lighten up this conversation just a little.

By this time, I had had enough greetings and cheer.

Several hours had passed and I never found my husband; not that I was exactly looking for him. (*Heck, I was too busy entertaining his relatives or relative wannabes.*) He can usually back himself in a corner with someone that talks as much as he does, and he is in heaven. *Didn't want to disturb his heavenly moment!* And knowing him like I do, it was probably about sports, politics, or the school system. I didn't want to talk about any of the above!

I walked around some more and found myself out on the porch, the front wrap around porch that is! *Mm*…what's that over there in the corner? I spied a big punch bowl, and it looked awfully full. Could it be? Could it be the right kind of punch for me? I decided to go take a look.

Over my shoulder I could see that more and more people were coming out to the porch. Were they coming outside because they were intolerable of the ice box, or were they looking for the wonderful beverage that I was looking for? I thought I would stick around and see but not before I went over to that punch bowl. As I sacheted over to my awaiting beverage, my sister-in-law Lenora came out onto the porch.

Lenora looked like she had had all she could stand too! She had that deer in the headlights look, you know, totally over smiling, greeting, hugging, and standing around that refreshment table. She was up to her eyeballs in mini pecan pies, cheese straws, chocolate dipped strawberries, crabmeat quiche, asparagus rolls, and salted nuts. (And enough "gas" to last her all week!) *Shut my mouth!*

Well, I looked at her and she looked at me!

"Let's see what's in that punch bowl; I heard Matilda spiked it!" we both said.

Matilda was a cousin and the daughter of that sweet little ninety-year-old lady that didn't know my name. Over we went and put the ladle in that marvelous liquid and found the biggest cup that we could find. It barely made it in the cup before we had the first swig down. Thank the Lord for Cousin Matilda! Let the reunion begin!

Lenora and I stayed out on that porch for a while, and then we stayed some more. All this time the porch kept filling up with people that didn't seem to know each other. Everyone started off standing around with their hands folded, quiet, looking around like they were lost. But as soon as they saw Lenora and I lightning up a little and really enjoying that punch, they decided to follow suit. Pretty soon had a little party going, and the inside of the house was clearing out fast.

Well, I finally found my husband after the porch had gotten so crowded, because everyone was moving outside. He motioned for me to come over and join him, so I just gave him that wild-eyed looked and pretended that I was looking for the bathroom! *Good cover!* I thought to myself. He was standing in the corner with who is that? And he almost seemed trapped, but I was not going to get him out of it! Not just yet!

He had brought me here against my will, and I was going to make him pay for his sins! So I went out the back door, around the side of the house, and back to the porch where the punch bowl was. It seemed like a larger party had started in the last few minutes, and I was determined to join in! Gonna make this reunion the best I have ever had.

We stayed out on that porch for quite some time before my husband and Lenora's husband finally showed their faces. By the time they showed up, we were so happy and cheerful that we had met every person on the porch, had drug the rest of the people from inside the house out to the porch, and had taken that elegant buffet and its goodies and placed them all over the place. Everyone was having such a good time that they forgot that they too had been forced to come here. *And it ain't just a coincidence either!*

So the next time, honey, that you get asked to go to a family reunion against your will, just go politely with your spouse, but be sure to raid your cabinet before you go! It makes it much more tolerable, and also you won't care if the little precious aunt calls you by the wrong name or not, and if the little old man shows up and it's not even the right party!

Here's cheers to you, ya'll! And the next time you go to a family reunion, take along a set of earplugs, sunglasses, and your favorite, well-behaved dog and stand near that punch bowl. No one will ever bother you and you can sip to your hearts content.

HOUSEWORK AIN'T ROCKET SCIENCE

Have you ever heard anyone say that houses clean themselves? *Absolutely not!* Have you ever heard that it takes a great deal of education to clean a house, even rocket science? *Absolutely absurd!* Well, in my family's case, you would think that all of the above apply! Ha! Then I think that most of the country is guilty of thinking that.

I think that God made women to clean up houses! No, really.

Have you ever seen a man or father of the household and the kids clean up a house while the woman or mother of the household sits in an easy chair, flips channels, and drinks a beer! If you have, I want her name and number so I can give her a high five!

My family obviously has not been educated formally on how to clean a house. And the more I think about it, the more I think that housecleaning or house *"work,"* as I call it, requires a formal education, a whole lot of common sense, and a little bit of energy. All qualities, except for the formal education, are what my family lacks. I tried to be a good teacher, but obviously I am not effective. Must need a rocket scientist.

Well, maybe we can start with a few chores and build from there. Probably should call them Housework 101, for beginners, or for the lazy, noncommittal, don't care people that live in my household or might live in yours. This might seem a little farfetched, maybe mean, but you know it's the dang truth.

Let's start with dishwashing or cheating and using the dishwasher. Do you think they would know how to do this without having to be taught? No! They must be prompted by good ole Momma leaving a note. I find that it is not possible unless it is written on a piece of paper in my handwriting, and at the end there is XOXO. Voicemails don't work, telling them doesn't work, and leaving everything dirty and all over the sink and cabinets doesn't work. They will just get out the paper plates!

And...there is never any dishwashing liquid unless I buy it. And LORD of mercy, they wouldn't know how to buy dishwasher soap. One reason the dishwashing liquid runs out is that my kids use it to wash their cars and leave it in the shop. Can't even bring it back in the house! Or they leave it in the carport, and it never sees the shop or the house or makes it back under the sink.

The next chore that they must be reeducated on is vacuuming. *Rather, educated!* I don't think in twenty-one years of marriage that my husband has ever learned to turn on a vacuum cleaner, or learned how to take it out of the closet. That would be too taxing and require too much brainpower! He would let the dirt get six inches deep in the house before he would consider it. But he will occasionally mention that there was an awful lot of cat litter or dog hair on that rug to me and look at me with concerned eyes. And

I will look at him with a *"eat dirt and die"* look, but I would never say it! But just keep prompting me!

The kids do fair with the vacuuming, you know the XOXO thing? Also, slipping them a few dollars for doing it because I am tired of looking at it and ready to kill them doesn't hurt either. But the farthest point for them is usually their room. They don't see the hall, the stairs, or any place else in the house. They also, like my *"uneducated"* husband, don't see past their immediate environment and would live in the six inches of dirt with him!

Bed making is a scream! My kids think that because they get back in it within twenty-four hours, what's the point? My son took his top sheet off and slept on top of the coverlet that I had put on. His clean linen would be sitting at the foot of his bed for a while before he took a notion. My daughter never makes her bed unless it is a holiday or I gave her *"the look"*!

"But what's the point?" she says. Now where have I heard that? They must pass notes!

Kids are something, aren't they? I guess when we have them; they are really carbon copies of us. Probably our parents wanted to strangle us a good bit of the time or thought very long and hard about it! And screamed at us so loud when we were growing up that all the neighbors could hear them; and we didn't live that close like we do now. I guess we reap what we sow, so I am getting what I deserve, from how I didn't do for my momma and daddy. And I am going to curse them tenfold for what my kids are now doing to me.

Getting back to the housework: dusting is also something that no one in this household thinks to do! I would like to see the actual color of the furniture that I have once in a while, and you can do this by dusting. All you do is get a rag or a soft cloth and just run it over the furniture. Or you can get one of those new-fangled gadgets that promise swifter dusting, and cheat a bit, but it does save a lot of time. When I was growing up, it was an old baby diaper and a can of lemon Pledge. I could go through a whole can in two days, and I could smear my name in all the furniture. A little too much, don't you think?

Well, my kids never dust unless I yell, or did yell. Now that they are older, I just sit the duster on the bottom of the stairs, and they walk around it for a few days, might take it upstairs in about a week or never. If it finally gets upstairs, they sit on the floor of their room and it sits some more. By the time they get around to dusting, the furniture is so thick with dust that the color looks faded. *Lazy kids!* And I should just *shut my mouth*, but you know I won't!

My husband, on the other hand, doesn't know what a dust rag is! He has his own den area and a little table by his couch that is black. And guess what black does? It gets dirty and dusty very quickly. I noticed that there are drink rings on it, fingernail clippings, used popsicle sticks, coffee cups, wadded up paper, pencil eraser dust, etc., and he will still wait until I clean it up. And yells or speaks loudly to me if I do clean it up and if I move things, like the channel changer or his cell phone charger. All I have to do is open a drawer and there it is, but I guess that's rocket science too!

Another thing that ticks me off is the lack of my family to want to clean the bathrooms! You could especially sandblast the kids' shower, because they never clean it! *Ew!* I provide all of the cleaning supplies for it, but they fight as to who is going to do it. I went up there one day, and there was a nice green ring in the toilet. Well, I would have liked to swab that thing and send it for a culture. They never clean their sink and never clean the mirror behind the sink! I have a pet peeve about nasty toothpaste spit on the mirror and no one minding to wipe it off. Looks like a snowstorm after a while, because no one bothers to clean it! And how in the world do they see their face in the mirror? But they seem to manage!

And the bathroom floor and the other floors in the house? Why, I don't think they know that a mop has been invented. You know the thing with a long handle and a sponge on the end? Yeah, that thing that is propped in the corner? You take the mop, you get a bucket, fill it up with water and floor cleaner, and away you go. And the magic thing is, you put the mop in the bucket, wring it out, and put it on the floor. Mopping 101!

And guess what? All my ever-loving family failed this course.

I have never seen any of them go near it, much less pick it up and use it! *Duh!* I think they think the floors clean themselves; another one of these rocket science excuses!

All in all, I think my family is incapable of learning the rocket science of housekeeping, or it is a selective disability or just plain *"I ain't doing it!"* laziness. Whatever it is, it still remains a problem to get them to participate in my fine art of housekeeping, so I continue to nag, remind, leave notes with the XOXO on it, call, leave voicemails, text message, and write it in the dust on the furniture and the smudge on the refrigerator door. Do they get the hint? *Sometimes.* Or they just pretend they have a disability and want forgiveness for not doing it!

So I will continue to do the motherly/wifely thing and try to keep the household from being condemned by the health department, and worse being evil-eyed by my own momma. You see, you really can eat off of her floors, and she has many times. But her life is keeping her home neat and tidy, and I be dern if it will be mine! So maybe it's not so bad that my house isn't the most tidy or clean, I have a smudge here and there, and you can see cat litter and dog hair on my rugs. But I do have another life outside this house, and it's called sanity, and I am proud of it!

So here's to ya'lls clean house and insanity/sanity! And to all those lazy family members that we all have that seem to be unteachable but actually might be a little smarter than we are, because we do the housework and they wiggle out of it. Maybe we ladies need to get on their side. *Nah! Couldn't stand it.* You know we have to nag somebody or something; it's the Southern way!

Amen!

I CARRIED MY "DRAWERS" THROUGH CENTRAL PARK!

This is another little bit of New York City humor, and my daughter Kelli will scream when she reads this. But this is my book, and I'm going to write about it because I can!

She and I went to NYC for four days in January and walked our legs off, literally. She had never been to the Big Apple, and I took a lot of pride or rather some insanity to take her there and show her the sights. Not that I don't love my daughter, but when you get two just alike women and force them together for four days in the same room, sharing a bathroom, and one is euphoric in the morning and the other doesn't talk for two hours and will glare at you when you do, I think you can just about draw your own conclusions.

We went to a lot of the touristy sites, such as Rockefeller Center, Macy's, Empire State Building, Wall Street, China Town, etc. We tried to see a lot of the NYC icons before we decided to do some serious shopping. Not that we had a lot of money to do that, mind you, or a lot of luggage space, but we did manage to try to clean up a couple of stores, and one of them was having a huge sale: Good ole Vicky's Secret! *(Name change, honey!)*

Why did we pick this store since we have and do have access to plenty of them? We don't know, I guess it was the huge *Sale* sign that was in the window and the fact that it was bigger and better than any one that I had ever seen, and you know how Southern women, or any woman for that matter, like a bargain.

Well, we went into that store, and glory be, it was full of sale tables full of underwear. Every kind of lace thing that you could imagine and a ladies' dream! My daughter and I went as fast as we could to every table that had a half off sign on it like it was our last feeding frenzy. Panties, bras, thongs, etc.; we poured through them all! Or as a lady would say, undergarments or as my Grandma would say, *"drawers."* My grandmother wouldn't recognize the "drawers" of today, she would be mortified.

I did say mortified! *Sometimes I am too!* Some of this so-called underwear, doesn't have six inches of material in it, and goes by the nickname of dental floss. Why in the world would somebody want to wear something that doesn't cover up a thing, and sits in your *"crack"?* Sorry … couldn't resist that one! Or these bras that have all this gel and padding in them that make you look four sizes bigger than you are? Well, I guess that's the point if you weren't blessed with it already. But in certain situations, the surprise is on the person at the other end of that equation. *Figure it out, honey!*

After an hour or two of pouring over these finds, we selected our favorites, purchased them, and we were given a bag that was as big as a piece of luggage to put them in. (Kelli had ½ yard of material, and I had two.) Looked like a big advertisement billboard to me. Had "Big Semi-Annual Sale" on it and could be seen a mile away! Not just this, when you have a sale like that and everything is half off, it just means that you buy twice as much. *Do the math, honey!*

We then left this fine store with satisfied *"bargain"* smiles on our faces and headed for the subway station with our giant bag. Bop, bop, bop we went down the street, bag of underwear in our hands. Little did we know how much trouble this bag would cause us in the long run or rather my daughter thought it did.

To the subway station we went, with our bag, and managed to get through the gate without tearing it. I handed the bag to Kelli and she handed it back to me. Why, I thought? It didn't occur to me at the time, but it was a little loud. Not subtle, but screaming through the subway station. At least she thought so.

We took the subway to the 86th stop and got off. We then walked two to three blocks to Central Park and decided to try to find some of the landmarks. Bag still in tow, on my arm, swaying in the wind, and crying out to everyone that passed by. "Semi-annual sale, semi-annual sale!" Carrying my "drawers" through Central Park was becoming a little bit of a chore and an embarrassing one for Kelli. *Heck, I'm too old to care about such things*!

Around and around we went, through the park and finding our landmarks. Walk, walk, walk, rest, put bag down, pick bag up, walk, walk, walk, and away we went. We figured by the time we had cleared most of the hurdles in that park that we had walked about two-three miles in the cold with our pocketbooks and with that giant *"sale"* bag. Figured we had advertised for half the population in New York by the time we had gotten to this point.

We decided to take some pictures beside one of the famous fountains that is in the park by the boathouse. Disappointedly, the fountain was bone dry, but we decided to take pictures anyway. *Who the heck cares, you can't see the water anyway!* Well, Kelli perched herself on the side of the fountain wall, struck a pose, and pulled that big bag up so I could snap the two of them. The bag took up one side of the photo and Kelli the other. I thought to myself, w*on't forget this photo!*

We walked and walked and walked some more, and it was way past lunchtime. Now you know that a Southern girl has a certain time frame to eat lunch, but doesn't everybody? My stomach was literally growling, and I wanted something to eat. But there ain't no vending machines in Central Park in the middle of nowhere, and some of the things were closed since it was the middle of the winter. *Bummer!*

Well, I did not fret, and remembered that glorious restaurant that sits on the west lower corner of the park—the beautiful Tavern! We weren't exactly dressed for the occasion, and we had been walking for several hours. Our hair was tousled, our cheeks were red, our shoes were a bit dirty, plus we had on *"car-washing clothes"* except for our designer coats and pocketbooks. Kelli's jeans were fashionably ripped and had old paint stains on them. I don't even remember what pants I had on, but I didn't care at this point. I was cold, hungry, and needed a potty, and I was not going to be halted by my appearance or that huge bag full of "drawers."

We went to the back of the restaurant and took a peek, or rather I did, and then I motioned for Kelli to follow me to the front of the building.

"I'm not going in there!" she said.

And I said, "Oh come on, and yes you are!"

She shot me one of those *eat dirt and die* looks, but I kept on walking. Right around to the front door of the place and in we both went and with that big semi-annual sale bag.

"Mom, I'm not dressed, and I'm embarrassed to go in here." I just kept walking. Around and around until I got to the maitre'd station.

"Two for lunch, please," but I should have said for three. Kelli, the bag, and me! "My money will spend just like someone's that has a suit on!" I told her and walked to the table. Kelli kept shooting me these looks and snorting until she sat down and noticed that there were some other *"not so dressed up"* people in there.

"But Mom, they aren't carrying this huge bag either."

"Who cares, Kelli?"

The waiter seated us in the middle of the restaurant and luckily there was a wall there to hide that dang bag. We both took our coats off, and I gave Kelli my scarf to dress her "car-washing" shirt up a little bit. I tried to hide my shoes under the table so no one would pay attention to them. Not really, just wanted to put it in here so it sounds like I was little embarrassed. *Not!*

We had a fine lunch at the Tavern and a fine bill to go with it! *Not really!* I will pay for anything as long as I get good service and good food. And I got both of them there, and then some. That bag just sat behind that wall and didn't bother anybody, because it was just about supper/dinner time, and there were only a few people in there, or rather they had been there since lunch, and it wasn't to order extra dessert! *Shut my mouth!*

We finished our meal, put our coats back on, and picked up our pocketbooks and that humongous bag that hit every table on the way out. Kelli seemed to walk a little faster than me to make a beeline for the exit, but I just took my time and waltzed out, because I didn't know how long it would be before I got to return to this fine place. *Probably wouldn't bring the bag back though!*

We left the restaurant and went back out into the streets of Central Park. Pretty quiet out here, one cab, no manned horse and buggies, a few pedestrians, but that was it. We hit the sidewalk and headed to 5th Avenue, me, Kelli, and the bag. We reached the avenue and decided to find that nearest subway station, which was a few blocks away, and it was getting a little cold.

Have you ever tried to carry a big bag like that when your hands are freezing? We managed! Kelli carried it for ten minutes and then we would switch. All the while advertising again for New York City. And you know when people see those bags; you know they know what's in it. It's definitely not a new pair of jeans or a whole lot of reading to do.

Oh well, who cares? I'm getting too old to care about such little trivial things such as a big bag that advertises underwear. Heck, everybody wears it, at least one time or another. But, if they don't, they won't pay attention to the bag or the advertisement anyway! But I bet in this cold NYC weather their tush is a little frostbitten. Now I will *shut my mouth,* and call it on this one.

Happy sale shopping ya'll!

I'M MIDDLE-AGED,
and I HAVE EARNED CELLULITE

We have discussed some things about middle age at the beginning of this book, but it is so near and dear to my heart, that I think it deserves a chapter of its own. I don't see anything wrong with it, in fact, I rather like it, and I think I have earned every blessed thing that it has given me: wisdom (*my kids would beg to differ*), gray hairs, bad knees, weakening eyesight, short temper, and cellulite, to name but a few.

Let' take the last, but not least, and talk about good ole cellulite! That *"cottage cheese"* described stuff that plants itself nicely on your butt, thighs, and anywhere else it decides to go to. It plants with a stronghold that a sandblaster couldn't take off. Forget the creams, cellulite pills, spot reducing exercises that promise you miracles that will take the stuff away! They don't work, because I've tried them all, and after all that, the stuff just looks at me and giggles. *Yeah it does!* Cause while I'm using the miracle drugs, creams, and exercises, I might have a cocktail or two, and everything giggles before I'm done. With the cocktails that is!

Being middle-aged, though, I say that I have earned

the right to have cellulite and not be so dang obsessed with taking it away.

I have these *"git rid of cellulite cravings"* when I see those perfect gals in those diet pill/drink/shake/food ads that don't seem to have any cellulite anywhere. (Those pictures are air brushed, so there!) I probably would look good too half naked, if my entire body was painted a special color of "flesh" and the computer would take off many inches here and there! Mind you, that's a whole lot of inches, but who's counting?

I have tried about every diet known to man and woman, and then some. Some I have just made up! The best diet I have found for me besides taping my mouth shut or eating cardboard, is to count points! But my points may not be the kind of points that are recommended. I would like the chocolate raspberry brownie for breakfast from *Kudzu* bakery times two, please, and that will take away over half of my daily total of points. So I just eat a bowl of lettuce and drink water the rest of the day, to get my total points. Not exactly a healthy diet or one to boost my metabolism. It really just gives me a sugar rush in the morning, makes me sleepy by noontime, and then I starve the rest of the day. But, I did like I was supposed to and counted my points! *Bummer, huh?*

The other diets I have tried are the high protein/low carbohydrate diet. I eat meat all day and salad, drink water, and can't have any fruit or carbs. This diet usually doesn't last that long, because the memory of that brownie still lingers. *And guess what?* I usually find a way to go to that bakery and get that brownie. Then it's back to the brownie diet, lettuce and water.

So much for willpower!

Getting back to cellulite, my permanent companion. I've tried every kind of exercise to spot reduce. Hah! If you think about it, that would look kinda weird if it did work. Fat thighs and a skinny butt! It just doesn't work that way. Might as well be fat all over so everything will match. Slow fat reduction all over so that you won't look asymmetrical or just plain stupid. *I need to shut my mouth!*

Exercise and more exercise. I have done so many squats and deep knee bends that I've given myself arthritis in both knees, and they click when I walk. *And guess what?* I haven't spot-reduced and the "cheesy" crap is still there. Now what do I do about my clicking knees? No diet, exercise, or willpower will take that away.

This is just a side effect of all my work of trying to get rid of this cellulite.

I think I'd rather have it than clicking knees!

Another thing that I have seen to get rid of cellulite is *"special"* creams and lotions that you rub on, and they are guaranteed to work. *Horse hockey!* They promise if you rub them in twice a day the cellulite will disappear. Well, I almost bought some of this stuff but decided against it. I've also heard of rubbing coffee grounds on your thighs to get rid of it. Think I heard that Cindy Crawford used to do this. And you don't see any cellulite on her either. Probably never had any to start with!

I don't think I want to put Maxwell House or my good Starbuck's coffee grounds on my butt and thighs, so that idea is a goner too! I'll just drink the coffee and hope that the coffee effect will make its way to where I want it to go too. But who makes up this stuff? It must be somebody that has no cellulite, has a lot of time on their hands, and has a dang good way of convincing us desperate middle-aged women that these tricks will work and make a fortune.

But for now, I'm middle-aged and loving it—cellulite and all. Heck, I said before that I've earned all of it. Gray hair too! I'm not ashamed of any of it. I wouldn't trade the knowledge and the wisdom that I have earned in my years, for any 25-year-old's brain. Didn't *Time Magazine* say that the brain was not developed until this age? (*That's what's wrong with them!*)

As for the cellulite, I'll make peace with it too and learn to tolerate it. LORD knows it ain't going anywhere unless I sandblast it or have liposuction like one of my relatives, or several of them, for all that I know. If I really get desperate I can starve myself and live on lettuce and water for a while, or a protein diet. But in the back of my mind that chocolate raspberry brownie times two from Kudzu keeps calling my name, and I'll have to give in. Who cares about cellulite anyway, especially when I'm savoring every last morsel of that delectable brownie?

So all you non middle-aged girls, keep on exercising and dieting till you're as thin as a waif! If you don't know what a waif is, look it up, if you're brain is developed. Have a perfect cellulite free butt and thighs with very little effort.

I still have my brownies! *And there ain't nothing better!* And you did know that chocolate is a natural aphrodisiac, makes you look ten years younger, gives you the energy of an athlete, the mind of a genius... and if you believe this, you'll fall for anything, won't ya!

So here's to middle age, and I'm loving every minute of it!

WHY I MIGHT PREFER DOGS TO MEN!

Some might say that is one of the most unkind things I could possibly say, 'cause it ain't true and why in the world would you prefer a canine to an actual human being? I'll tell you right now that this is absolutely true, and here's why!

First of all, I do love all the men in my life: my channel-flipping husband, my son, my Daddy, my brother, etc. etc. Now…this doesn't have a thing to do with love, well maybe just a little bit. It's just that the company of a beloved canine might be very much preferred to being in the company of some or all of these men.

Let's take my brother or my Daddy for instance. They see me, they give me a hug, they talk for a little while, and then they are silent; usually to stare at the television. *(Another technology flaw!)* They will sit there, looking around or staring, shifting their tush in the chair or the couch, picking or wiping their noses, pick up a magazine, lean forward, look at me some more, make small talk like, "What are you doing now!" And I'll think to myself, *watching you do all of the above!* And then they repeat the process. That's usually the highlight of the visit. Now I know that is unkind, but it's the truth. Now tell me it ain't so if you've really watched your beloved relatives!

Now my son might be a little different. He won't stay still long enough to be in my company for very long. Always fidgeting and seldom focused for long. He usually says, "Hi Mom," and gives me a hug, and then away he goes. And it's usually to the computer to play a game or watch a movie or check his "*My Personal Space.*" Then he will come away from outer space in a while, come by me and say "later!" and then leave. End of a long conversation. Ha! Or I might get a pat on the back and then "later!" So far a very bonding experience!

This one is interesting; it's my channel-flipping husband. He gets up in the morning with a grunt, no talk, and staggers into the kitchen and makes coffee. Comes and gets my beloved dog Megan and takes her out. Comes back, takes a shower, goes back to the kitchen, and settles down with his paper. And don't you dare take the "local" section before he has a chance to read it and to work the Sudoku puzzle. More coffee, breakfast, more grunts, and he is ready to go to work. "Bye," quick kiss, and out the door he goes. But not before he says "lock the door" before he closes it. Wow! What a morning! And such interesting conversation again!

Pretty boring up until this point? It does get better. When I wake up in the morning, my beagle Megan is usually right by my side and waking up with me. She has been in the same spot all night, and if I move she does too! Quite a cuddler she is, and always greets me every morning with a gentle lick or two or three.

She even will put her head on my neck if my head is turned and try to lick my face. *How sweet it is!*

Now honestly, have you ever heard of a man doing this? Not wanting a man to lick my face, but a kiss would be very appropriate. Ah never mind...let's just finish the story.

After Megan goes out with my husband and has her breakfast, after she has waited patiently, she usually comes back to bed with me. Snuggle and lick some more! That's special to me! No grunts, no snorts, just likes being close to me. And that is her conversation. We have this canine to mistress understanding, she and I, and it's our own special relationship that only we understand.

Then we usually go into the kitchen and have coffee and the paper together. She usually sits at my heels or gets on the couch and watches me. She wants to know where her momma is at all times. After this ritual, we go back to my room, and I get dressed for work. She sits patiently on the bed and waits for me to finish and doesn't move. Do you think one of the men in your life would do that? I think not, and if you say "yeah," I'm gonna say, "the heck you say!" And it must be a new relationship. Cause after any relationship has a little age on it, and you know I am the expert, you no longer get a great thrill out of watching your partner do anything: eating, sleeping, watching TV, putting their socks on, picking their teeth. You get my drift now, or should I keep going?

As I leave for work, I open the blinds for her to see out the window. Megan will usually sit on my bed all day while I'm at work to wait patiently for me to come home. And when I finally do pull into the driveway after a long day at work, I can hear her excited barks before I get out of the car.

When I do put the key in the lock and open the door after a long day at work, always and I mean always, she is the first one to greet me at home. Always with excitement, a wagging tail, and more gentle licks to give me. Then she wants to jump in my arms and give me a *doggie hug*. And I am more than happy to receive her attention and give her the attention that she needs in return. *Ain't nothing like it*!

So, when I say I might prefer dogs to men, I hope the men really won't take it personally. *'Cause it ain't a personal thing*! Dogs are just loveable, gentle creatures that are put on this earth for one purpose, and that is to love their master or mistress and receive it in return. Unconditionally! You can have a bad day and don't want to talk to anyone or anything, but I bet when you see that dog coming toward you, I bet your attitude changes. You can't help it!

If your spouse, significant other, or any of the other men in your life met you at the door like your canine "love" does, I bet you'd have a very different opinion of them. *Now wouldn't you?* I think sometime, heck a lot of the time, that all of us could take some compassion lessons from our wonderful canines. I've never seen them walk about with a scowl on their face, a downright nasty attitude, or bark and bite when you want to be nice to them. Just doesn't happen in most cases.

So if you don't agree with me or really want to challenge me with this, and you do have a dog, look around and really *see* what happens. Or if you don't, maybe you need to really think about getting one. I tell that to people, and those that don't have dogs just laugh and say *"no thanks"* a lot of the time.

But I consider myself the lucky one with this dog, and I am glad that I have continued to be very much a dog lover and have been lucky to have had many of these incredible creatures in my life. I think they do contribute to me being a happier more playful person, because this canine is not just an ornament to me, but very much a part of my existence.

So don't take yourself too seriously, spend time with a dog, and then you can make the decision whether you'd like to spend more time with them or with the men in your life. Or whether you'd like gentle licks/ kisses or grunts at the breakfast table? I bet I know who you'd choose!

Now it really is time to *shut my mouth!*

WHEN GOD CREATED GROCERY STORES, HE DIDN'T ASK ME!

Now, just what did I mean by that? Everyone has grocery stores: little towns, big towns, large metropolitan cities, little podunk towns, just about any town with some size to it have one. But when they were in the stages of creation, I wasn't even in the equation, but I could tell them a thing or two about building them.

Grocery stores are usually places that I dread at some time or another. And probably the reason that I dread them is because the way that most of them are built and the aggravation that I have to go to get to one, go inside, and get what I want. Now, if you say that you have never felt that way, well I'll just take you along with me the next time I go, and I bet I can change your mind! I'll just tactfully point out some things along the way and make a big *"hoo hoo"* about nothing, if you get my drift.

Good ole grocery stores! Those big buildings that we all hate to go to, but let's face it, we gotta eat. Or we can go out everyday, but our pocketbooks would be depleted in a hurry. Okay, back to the initial point!

As soon as you drive up, you have to find a parking spot. And this usually takes a few minutes if you want to get the right spot. The right spot for me just happens to be the one that is closest to the store and not a half-mile away. I also hate it when I do find a decent spot and some *"hair brain"* parks his limo between two spots so I don't have room to get into it. And then I have to go look some more. And if it's raining, there are big pot holes in the parking lot, so they fill up with water, and I step in them (usually with my good shoes or favorite heels) on the way in and on the way out. No fun!

Once I do manage to get inside, then it's time to pick a cart. I must be cursed, but those carts hang up when they are slung together, and I have a hard time getting them to pull apart. And I must be double cursed, 'cause every time I get a cart the wheels squeak and they won't roll straight like they ought to. I think those carts have a pact, and when they see me coming, they automatically become dysfunctional. "Here she comes! Let's drive her nuts!" Every time this happens, every time! And no, I'm not just being a girl about it.

Okay, I've got the squeaky cart with the bad wheels, and now it's time to drive it around the store. Drive is so the correct word! Why can't they keep those carts oiled or take a screwdriver or wrench to them once in a while? Did it ever occur to anyone that these things do break after the 500th customer uses them? Duh! Or if they plow into a car, because they have escaped the cart return?

Now…let's go through the deli aisle, then the fruits and vegetables. And why can't they put plastic bags for your produce on every table. And why can't they keep them filled! I'm going to spend $5.00 for four tomatoes, and I have to walk over an aisle to get a freaking bag. And a twist tie? Forget it! I'll just get the pre packaged ones and pay $7.00. Not really, but that ticks me off!

Then I'll head toward the canned vegetables and salad dressing aisle. And I am going to have to play "rock, paper, scissors" with this little elderly couple to see who gets to push their buggy through the aisle without having to wait. *Dang it!* She's got coupons and he doesn't like the brand, and they are discussing the nickel difference between the two brands that they are looking at. LORD give me patience, please!

"Excuse me … excuse me?"

They both must have hearing aides that aren't turned on!

"Excuse me?"

Finally they hear me and move at least an inch so I can get by. *Bless them!* And I never did get any vegetables or salad dressing.

Around I go to the next aisle and the next. Dodging moms with kids, other little elderly couples, or little old ladies, and maybe a kid by themselves, and they are trying to climb on the shelves like a set of monkey bars. Store stockers are trying to keep the shelves stocked, and they have a whole truckload of things in the middle of the aisle. Why can't they do that at night, like they used to do?

"Excuse me?" I say again. But at least they hear me the first time. What did I come down this aisle for? I can't for the life of me remember. Oh well, I'll probably remember when I leave the store and start home, like I usually do.

Well, let's go to the frozen food aisle. Now if things are half price or on sale, the freezer cases look like Belk when they have a fifty percent off sale. Stuff everywhere! And things are usually picked over when I get there. Where's the stock boy when you need them? And why is the Whitehouse Cherry with Walnut ice cream always sold out when I get there? *Figures!*

This aisle is also a mini racetrack because it will only hold one cart/buggy, whatever you call it, beside the freezers, because there are displays in the center of the aisle. So who has to move when you meet up on this freezer aisle? Usually I do. I won't ask a little old lady or elderly couple to move; it ain't polite! I'll just move over to the other side to the refrigerator section. But if I meet a mom with two screaming kids that are misbehaving and terrorizing the other patrons, she can move, 'cause I ain't moving! The parking lot for her and those kids would be more like it! *Shut my mouth!*

Why can't they make these aisles reasonably bigger to accommodate the customers? What is the big deal? We come in here and spend a *"butt-load"* of money, and we all have to fight or bargain with each other over who is going to get down the aisle first. What is wrong with this picture? *Do the math, honey!*

Whew, made it this far without a stroke, so now I have to go to the meat section. This ain't so bad unless you have a sale, and you're trying to look over someone's shoulder to look at a piece of meat. And instead of moving their buggy over, they leave it next to the meat counter so you'll have to move it yourself, or kill yourself trying to see that piece of meat that is on sale. Ah, forget it; I'll just stick to fish this week! But the customers will probably block the seafood window with their cart/buggies too!

After I have had enough with shopping or rather wrestling this cart/buggy, little elderly couples that can't hear a word I'm saying, moms and screaming kids that are climbing on everything, sold out products, not enough room for two in the aisles, rude or brain dead customers; I decide to go and try to check out! This is what I really hate! I wrestle my cart to the front of the store and decide to put my life in my hands once again, and I'm already hanging by a shoestring.

Do I sound stressed? I probably am by this point. I have to find a line without ten people in it, even though there are five cash registers that aren't being used or rather no one is manning them. Now what is wrong with this picture? *Customer service, people!*

Don't you see the ticked off look on our faces? Doesn't it matter?

I guess not, because they only have two lines open! Ah!

So I pull up to line #2 since it only has about four ahead of me, and it looks like three of them have a lot of coupons. I stand in line for about a quarter of an hour and finally get to the scanner. I have to move around to the front of my cart/buggy to be able to put my purchases on the scanner. And there ain't enough room for a size ten woman to fit into a size four space to get between that cart and the candy display. I have to squeeze through, unload, and squeeze back. Now if I were a size larger, I would just be out of luck! No squeezing for me! That is another ridiculous way of building checkout aisles.

They must have been *"out to lunch"* when the architects designed them. But they keep building them the same way. Must be a little thing called *"Duh!* I didn't realize that, but it does saving a ton of money to do it that way. You can sit on the side of the buggy at the checkout counter and dip your hand into the candy display at the same time, and also take a few inches off your assets. *Had to be a man that designed this too!*

Enough of that, but I finally get all of my purchases scanned and the last one doesn't have a price on it. *Ah and that figures!* The cashier has to call someone from stock to come up to the register to get the item, to take it back to the aisle for a price check, and bring the item back. Bet the stock boy wished he could crucify the one that put the prices on them! So why don't they do it right the first time, moron? *Shut my mouth!* (I'm a little ticked by now, if you can't tell!)

Now it's time to pay for all of my purchases, after the delay with a price check. I get out my debit card and my store card, have to scan them both, put in a code, wait for the cashier to okay it, and it finally spits out my receipt and coupons. In case I want to come back again. A cold day…anytime soon or when my family is at home with their tongues hanging out due to starvation!

Well, I made it and in one piece! I have probably forgotten half of what I came for, but I don't feel like wrestling any more carts or any more people. Now I've got to get my groceries to my car, put them in the car, and can hopefully drive home without stopping at the nearest bar for a *"sedative"!* Just kidding! I don't come to the grocery store that often, because I manage to bribe my kids or my channel-flipping husband to come and do it. Dang it…there ain't anything in the Bible that says women are the only ones that can do the grocery shopping. *And I say Amen*! Now if God has asked me to help him create the design of the grocery store, I would have been much obliged. But you know, it probably was a man that designed it, and he didn't have a freaking clue! Now honey, you know this is true, and you know who does the majority of the grocery shopping?

Now I will say kudos to that, and we're going out for dinner tonight! And my non grocery-shopping husband is going to take me too! I have to get something for my pain and suffering, and you gals should take my advice and milk it for all it's worth. They'll never know the difference.

HECK FIRE
... *and* IT AIN'T *the* BEDROOM!

Probably not a nice assumption to make, but for all you middle-aged gals, I bet at least half of you agree with me on this! *Now, say it ain't so!* The bets on me!

What happens to people when they reach middle age, and today it hits around forty, and the fire starts to flicker a little? Heck, for all I know your bedroom fire is just about died down, if not extinguished. Take a fire extinguisher to it, and it would go out in five seconds flat! Pretty bad, huh?

What happened to the beginning stages of a new love relationship and the fire was burning hot? Kisses, hugs, love pats, caresses, flowers, jewelry, lets you pick the TV channel, opens the door for you, calls just to hear your voice, offers to help you, cooks for you, and looks so excited to see you! What happened to all of that? Probably started to die with the brain cells, but I'll just *shut my mouth* for now.

After living with someone for twenty-thirty years, I guess after a while, they do begin to look like a recording. Hey, but relationships should age like a fine wine, shouldn't they? Not sour and go rancid, at least not in this book!

Let's look at some examples on how *not* to let the fire go out of your relationship. And just to be fair, I have included both sexes:

1) When your significant other wants to go on a "just the two of you" romantic dinner, since your time is limited, don't take them to a sports bar!

This will probably not make the other part of this twosome happy, especially if they are not a sports fanatic. It may also cause you to get dirty looks from the other person, kicks under the table, snorts, fidgeting, and frequent trips to the bathroom due to sheer boredom. So this is probably not a good choice!

2) Don't wear flannel pajamas to bed!

This is probably not the best choice to bring out the *"beast"* in your significant other. It will just make him want to get out the sleeping bags and the tent. And the hound dogs! Want him to think about a boys' weekend, just wear this attire, unless its flannel lingerie, and he might think a little differently. I wonder what a camouflage bra would look like?

3) When you go to a restaurant, don't whip out a book or a newspaper to read!

That will probably kill any romantic intentions that you might have had. This also says to the other person *"you're not interesting enough."* That is just totally not done and will not make a long lasting impression on the other person. Boring! And this is totally rude, rude, rude and wants to make the other person want to slap you from across the table or at least think about it real hard.

4) Don't burp or pass gas in the other person's company!

A really big faux pas, also rather disgusting in a very big way! Never makes a lasting impression on anyone, but the smell does! It also says to the other person, "I don't give a dang!" Also a really big faux pas with my momma, and she would have swatted you on the fanny!

5) Don't go to bed with or walk around the house in curlers.

Not a very pretty sight and certainly not a sexy one. Your significant other will definitely not try to get romantic with a bunch of antennae on your head. Probably will put his eye out! Also might remind him of his mother! And that is not painting a pretty picture.

6) Don't wear "granny panties," even if you are one!

This is probably one of the unsexiest things that you can do. Wearing those "drawers" that go up to your navel or beyond, that are white cotton, and sag a little bit at the base of your tush. *Ugh!* Not exactly romance material! Sister, take those things and throw them away or use them for a dust rag! Now go buy you a pair of those sexy silkies or a thong! And I bet Vicky's Secret is having a sale.

7) Don't take your partial or your false teeth out in front of the other party.

Not only is this being gross, don't ever do this. Let them think you have a mouth full of teeth that are totally your own. And don't lay them down where the other party can see them. And don't tell stories about them like, my ex-girlfriend used to put this in her mouth when we were dating. Totally uncool and totally disgusting. The girlfriend was probably a winner too if she did this! So keep those choppers in your mouth!

8) Don't dye your hair when your partner is home.

Let them think your gorgeous mane is your own, and hide the box. Even if they know it, you don't have to advertise it. Medium, ash blonde, or fiery red should be your secret. Plus, it's not attractive to see gook all over your head with your hair plastered to it! It is a little scary, especially when you are doing just the roots. Freddie Kruger might be the only one scarier!

9) Don't stay glued to the plasma all day long until bedtime.

If you don't talk to the other person all evening, and then when it's time for bed, reach over and expect a prize, forget it, pal! You should have thought about that all evening when you were in *la la land*. The other party likes romance and foreplay, at least a little, not just right before you try to get a *"touchdown."* Each party realizes that they know what the other one is thinking, but this becomes the recording that I was talking about earlier, and pretty soon both parties are sick of it!

And last but not least, the 10th *no no*:

10) Don't try to grab a 5-minute "quickie" when the kids or teenagers are home and awake.

This is probably the most unsatisfying thing that you can do for at least one of the parties. Well, maybe give it a couple of more minutes. But one of the party members will walk away with a lot of frustration, especially if the kids are making a ruckus and are constantly banging on the door or looking for their parents. Nothing breaks the mood more than hearing the word "Momma or Daddy" at the top of a child's or teenager's lungs, or if the dog starts scratching on the door without ceasing. Pretty unromantic, huh!

Whew! This has made me tired and frustrated just thinking about all these ways not to take the romance out of your relationship! So what do you do to put some of the romance back? I am not a therapist or even a good person to give advice, but I'll give it a try, honey. I'm good at sticking my nose into other people's business, at least my family tells me that, so I'll give it a shot!

Let's see, for starters, be the right person and pick the right person. Be kind and sensitive to the other persons needs. Make time for romance. Ah horse hockey, I hear that recording playing and it's gonna play forever. You can't fight middle age, so you might as well enjoy it. So let him take you to a sports bar, eat, take his credit card and his car keys, and say you'll see him in a few hours. He's happy, you're happy, when you finish spending his credit card, go home, light some candles, and have a *"quickie"* and call it a day. Ain't no use in getting upset about a little thing like romance, at least not this stage in the game.

Now say amen and halleluiah to that! But if you

need anymore advice, tap me on the shoulder when you see me, and we'll take a trip to the bookstore together or go see one of my friends that has had about 4 husbands and let her give us some advice.

TRYING TO CONVERT *the* TELEMARKETERS

Telemarketers are some of the most aggravating people, in my opinion, and if I could crawl through the phone and, get my hands on them, I just might. Not literally, but I think about it a lot, especially when they call me at *all* the wrong times! If you are one of these people, I'll go ahead and apologize upfront, 'cause what I'm going to say is not nice. I realize you work for a company that takes delight in aggravating the pants off of America and almost off of this Southern gal.

It never fails, and you can beg to differ, but as soon as I am upstairs, sitting down to eat, doing what nature intended or taking a nap—guess who calls?

I usually run like a maniac to answer the phone, thinking, *something has happened to the kids, my mother or father, my husband*. You know what I mean? I'm afraid not to answer it, because I'm a little bit of a worrier, at least some of the time. Ah heck, all of the time.

My husband won't ever let the phone just ring, for all of those reasons that I just mentioned. Then why in the heck did we get an answering machine? We had an answering service through the phone company at one time, but we seldom retrieved our messages. We got a lot of flack from our friends and relatives, so we canceled it. Might as well, didn't answer it anyway! So why is it a catastrophe if we don't answer the phone now? We have a machine that we can hear answering the phone, hear the voice of the person calling, and hear what is being said, but he answers it anyway.

I got off the subject, so I'll get back to those telephone *"tie-er uppers."* When I do go answer the phone, after almost breaking my neck to get there, I get silence at least for a few seconds, which ticks me off! Then if I am crazy enough to stay on the line, I might hear, "Mrs. Doling?" And I know it's some dang telemarketer on the line. They never get my name right. And if I'm still crazy enough to answer them, I might say, "Yes?"

That was a mistake also, 'cause you never stay on the line with them. Never! It's just a cardinal rule! Okay, so I've gone this far I might as well continue. "Mrs. Doling, would you like us to ya da, ya da, ya da."

I can't believe I'm listening to this. So I put the phone down, go get a glass of iced tea, turn on the computer or go to the bathroom, and wondering if that nut is still on the phone when I do come back. *And you know what?* Sometimes they are. Or I might hear a very loud buzz. Probably trying to charge me for the call!

And why is that that these telemarketing companies always get people that you can't understand what they say'? I always have to have them repeat everything, and then just forget about it. I know these telemarketers are just as aggravated as I am trying to communicate with me, so I don't get why they still want to do this job.

Getting back to answering the phone and actually talking to them ... well that can be a big mistake. But if I really want to be mean, and Southern girls can have a mean streak, I just slam the phone down as soon as I get that few seconds of silence and laugh to myself because I have done it. My husband might look up at me between channels and say, "Who was that?"

"Just another telemarketer. Can't you tell by the way I slammed the phone down? Didn't slam it down the way I usually do when *your* friends call!" No reaction; told you he didn't pay attention to anything that I say.

My husband, on the other hand, borne and raised a Southern gentleman and likes to talk, will actually carry on a conversation with them. He'll let them have their say, and then he'll start asking questions. "Why do you want to know that, exactly what are you selling, who are you selling it for, where are you located?" and I look at him like he is nuts, and he still keeps on talking. He keeps talking, and I finally say to him, "Are you going to get off the phone or are you crazy? Or are you going to build a relationship with that telemarketer 'cause you have asked them every question under the sun, except who's your daddy?" And most of the time it doesn't faze him. 'Cause you see, it was not his idea to get off the phone, but mine. *Just like a man!*

After he finally gets off the phone after five-ten minutes, when it was *his* idea, I might decide to confront him about his lack of good sense! Nah ... it can wait for another day. Have to save up all the dumb things he does and give it back to him when he really does something stupid. Which is quite often by the way. *Shut my mouth!*

So I have to ask myself, why do these telemarketers continue this madness? Don't they ever get tired of getting hung up on, humiliated, and goodness knows if anybody ever buys anything from them due to their reputation. So why do they do it? Don't they realize that they can go to work at *Wally World* for probably the same money, plus benefits, and probably get to advance in the company? Instead they work for some deadbeat company that doesn't pay them anything, and they continually harass the rest of America and ruffle this Southern gal's feathers. *So what's up with that?*

Well, enough of that! Maybe I should have a heart and feel sorry for these unfortunate souls that have to work for a telemarketing company? We, or at least I, treat these people unkindly by slamming the phone down and not listening to a thing they have to say. I won't listen to their programmed speech, contribute to their commission, and make these companies rich! I don't have time for all of this time, 'cause I'm too busy trying to keep my husband off the phone.

So the next time they call, gently pick the phone up, wait the few seconds of silence, and ask them when they say "Mr. or Mrs. So and So," stop them, and make them listen to you. "Have you put in an application at Wally World or Mac-a-Doo's; do you want a respectful job, or do you want to be known as the telephone terrorist for the rest of your life?" If you get silence, maybe they are thinking about it, or maybe they are trying to find the place that they left off in their programmed speech. Nah...we couldn't get so lucky!

Instead, when they call, slam the phone down like I usually do! Smile at your husband and say, "Wrong number"! Then turn around and chuckle to yourself that you have at least stopped another telephone terrorist from calling your home until the next time!

But the next time I think I will be waiting with a whistle and an application to Domino's! And now I think I'll go to the mailbox to pick up my husband's subscription to *"Moron Monthly"* and dig my elbow in just a little bit deeper. But what good Southern gal would go a thing like that?

WHO ATE MY FAVORITE GIRL SCOUT COOKIES?

Every year I buy a batch of those wonderful cookies, not directly from a Girl Scout, but from one of the mothers at my work. She brings me the list, I check it twice and place my order once a year, just like Christmas, and I can't wait for my stash to arrive. And they don't get in a hurry, so I wait some more.

Well, this year, I finally got my wonderful cookies. I got four boxes: one chocolate chip, one thin mint, one lemon, and one box of my absolute favorite—*Samoas*. One box and one box only of those wonderful coveted cookies that I had waited all year for. One box! One box to take home and maybe share with my family.

I took those cookies home, put them all on the counter, and then left there. Big mistake! I was thinking that my family would come home and see them and might open a box or two and help me to eat them. I certainly hadn't planned on eating any of them except for those coveted Samoas. The others could sit on the counter all year, but not those. Those were special and loved by everyone in this household. And you would think your family would be a little courteous and share the cookies, not try to hoard them one by one.

The next time that I went out to the counter, that I remember, one of the boxes of thin mints had been opened, half a roll had been eaten, and the wrapper had not been twisted back on. *Figures!* They never know how to put crackers or cookies back of any kind. In their thinking, they just leave them on the counter exposed to the air and take a chance that they won't go stale or get soggy. But in their defense, I don't think they have a freaking clue! No one in their whole life has taught them how to rewrap a cracker or cookie wrapper. Maybe screamed at them how to do it, but not gently taught them how to do it. *I don't know why I made that point!*

The next time I remember going out to the counter to see if they had unwrapped anything and not wrapped it back up, I counted only three boxes of cookies left. Lemon, thin mints, and chocolate chips were all here. The Samoas were not. And I know good and well that they could not have eaten that whole box of cookies since I last looked on that counter. No crumbs, no nothing, too neat, no evidence, something's up!

My husband came into the kitchen, and I pounced on him as soon as his foot hit the linoleum.

"Did you take those Samoas?"

"What?"

"You heard me!"

"I haven't seen any Samoas."

"I had four boxes of cookies on this counter and the Samoas are missing."

"I haven't had any cookies."

"Well somebody has, and they are missing."

"Don't look at me!"

"And why not, you're usually guilty."

I let him escape with his dignity, but not before he grabbed a handful of cookies, put them on a napkin, and lightly twisted the cookie bag back. *Dang it,* I thought to myself, *I guess they'll only get a little stale being put back like that.* I wonder who teaches these men. If it had been me, I would fail them all. Cookie Closure 101.

The next victim to come into the kitchen was my daughter, looking tired like she always does. Plus, she just got up from her long winter nap in the middle of the day.

"Have you seen my box of Samoas?"

She just looked at me with wild eyes, like don't talk to me for the next thirty minutes.

And this is a ritual with her. No talking at least for the first half an hour to one hour that she is up, because she will usually respond inappropriately. So with this wild eye response, I let it go. I didn't think she would have had the energy to eat a cookie, much less a whole box.

She turned and slowly fled the kitchen after getting a cup of coffee or rather ½ coffee and ½ French vanilla creamer. That would have been nice with those cookies! Ah forget it, she doesn't have the energy.

The next family member, and the only one left, to grace my presence and my kitchen, was my son. In a hurry as always, I asked him if he had seen the only box of Samoas that were on the counter?

"Nah, have you seen my jacket?"

"No, Josh, I haven't seen your jacket, but have you seen my cookies?"

"I gotta go, since I'm on duty at the chapel!"

Mind you he works for a church on some of his weekends. Ah hah I thought! Over avoidance and quick to run! I bet he knows what happened to those cookies, and I bet he took them to the chapel to share with the other young, supposedly honest men that work there. Dang cookie hoarders! And they probably have the whole box!

After Josh left, I kept looking at that counter, wishing I had a couple of Samoas to eat right now and someone was depriving me of it! But who? *I bet I could take a wild guess.*

I went all weekend and my box of Samoas never did appear and no one would fess up to it. Dang cookie hoarders, all of them. They probably ate the whole box in one sitting and didn't think I would notice. I bet they even buried the box in the backyard. A whole box, and I didn't even get one dang cookie. *I hope they all throw up!!* And I mean that with all my little self-centered heart.

Monday morning finally came, and I happened to see my sweet Girl Scout Mom in the hallway.

"Karen, have you got any more of those Samoas, 'cause I didn't get one of my own cookies. My family ate the whole freaking box!"

"Sure I do," in her sweet Southern voice.

You see, she is as Southern as I am, and she is from Virginia. Out she went and back she came with two boxes of those wonderful cookies. Mine, mine, mine! And my dang family was not even going to see me with them.

That night I went home, Josh was home from the chapel, Kelli was wide awake and not just up from a nap, and my husband was at home for dinner. You see, it is unusual for my husband to be home at night with all of us, but that's another story. Well, I brought up that box of Samoas again and asked sweetly if anyone had seen it. Out of the blue, my smirky son said, "Yes I did, and they were delicious!" and I wanted to lunge at him across the table. I gave him a very hard evil eye, my daughter laughed, and my husband looked like a deer in the headlights.

"Okay," I said, "you thought that was funny, huh?" "Did you realize that that was my favorite cookie, and that I only had one box? You could have eaten the other three, and I wouldn't have given a rat's behind. That one is my favorite and I did not get even one!" Dang cookie hoarders! I hope he has permanent cookie crumbs in his... ...

Silence, snicker, pout and immediate room exit by my two children. My husband just sat there and didn't say a word. Better not either, 'cause he knew I was ticked. Ain't nothing like a ticked Southern belle or a mad woman about anything.

Well, I still have those two boxes of Samoas in my desk at work, and I have no immediate plans to bring them home now or ever. *Ain't gonna share them either!* I'll be a little sneaky like my family and slowly bring them into the house. I will hide them someplace where they won't have a clue. Like near the household cleaning supplies or the toilet paper since they never go near the things.

So next year when the cookies go on sale, I will be the first in line or rather on paper. I will make sure that I get at least four boxes of Samoas for me and maybe one for my family. So when they come crawling to me when they have eaten theirs and know that I have four boxes, I will just smile will sheer delight and say, "yes, I have more, and they're good too! Sorry!" Or I'll just give them what's left of the roll that they forgot to seal. Stale cookies and all!   That's   the   breaks.   So don't ever take a Southern girl's cookies, especially if they are the annual Samoas.

And that ain't fiction, honey child, that's a fact!

CAN'T SLEEP?
WELL, ROLL OVER SO I CAN!

I don't know who is worse, me or my husband when it comes to trying to sleep at night. I don't think there has been one night in the last several years, or ever, that we have both gotten to go to sleep and stay that way all night. My memory is pretty good, but I am dang sure I don't know of a single night in the last decade.

My husband is a snorer by trade, and yes he could be a professional at it. He has snore tactics that are amazing and hits decibels that even a conductor would be proud of. And when he reads this, he's going to say "I do not!" and "Why did you put that in there, 'cause it ain't true!" So I will have to deal with him when the time comes, but it's my book and a long time before he will get around to reading this, so if I'm spreading lies about him, so be it! I know the truth and I have the tape recordings to prove it.

My dear ole husband and I have been married for going on twenty-two years. Have never been apart much, so we have spent many sleepless nights together and then one of us, mainly me, moves to the couch. My husband will usually try to go to bed first, unless I beat him there, and then by the time I arrive the concert has already started. We have bass, tenor, and soprano all in one! And it depends on which side of his body he is sleeping on.

I usually try to roll him over when he starts the "music," but changing his position only changes his pitch. If I want to try to find a tune that I can live with or rather sleep with, it may take a few times of pushing, shoving, elbowing, and rolling before I can tolerate it. This is usually accompanied by a "What? Huh! What are you doing? You woke me up!" And I'm thinking to myself, *So! But I don't want to fight with him in the middle of the night; I'll just wait until the morning.*

I just ignore all verbal contact for the time being and continue with my plan. After a few minutes of trying to get it right, it can become quite a workout. I know, 'cause I've got the muscle strains to prove it!

Now, if I am lucky enough to go to bed first, and this is usually my plan, I might get to fall asleep before he stumbles in, and I mean stumble. He usually sits on the side of the bed really hard, so hard as to make me lift up in the air a little, and then I bounce a few times before I come to a landing. Then he throws his feet on the bed, bumps some more, and maybe starts pulling the cover off of me. And usually by this time he has already woken me up if I was lucky enough to get to sleep to start with. *Dang it!*

Shift and wiggle, wiggle and shift some more, until I say that he gets into his nesting position. Now I am really awake! Then if he forgets to set the alarm clock, he will bounce a few more times before he gets the clock set then back to the nesting position again. I am almost ready to kick him completely out of bed by this time, since he has bounced me totally out of *my* nesting position.

And between him and the dog, which I forgot to mention sleeps with us every night, I have about twelve inches of mattress to sleep on. Our dog takes up the middle between us, and my husband takes up the left half side of the bed. *You do the math!* So if I really only have about a foot of bed to sleep on, the back position is totally out of the question, so it's the side for me.

After no more bouncing, then the concert will begin, and it ain't me! Then the turn over, "huh," elbows in the side, shaking, pushing, and calisthenics class begins. I literally have to work at being given the privilege of actually sleeping like a normal person. *It just ain't fair!*

So if this plan doesn't work, it's to the couch for me, and it is not the most comfortable thing in the world. But at least I have about two feet to sleep on and the back position is available. But usually I forget my pillow, and I have already closed the bedroom door that is squeaky, so not to disturb my husband and his concert, I opt for a decorator pillow. And let me tell you, honey, these ain't comfortable.

Have you ever tried to sleep on anything or even taken a nap on anything that has a button, lace or decorative balls on it? Have you ever seen your face after you have? You look plum scary, with indentations and all. Looks like you've had a bad dermabrasion!

Oh well, enough of that, but I forgot to mention that our dog will sleep with only me. And that's okay, 'cause I can't sleep without her either. It's something how I've bonded with this canine, and we're not just dog and owner, but she's one of my children as well. And she snores too, but that's another story!

So I put my dog on the end of the couch, I'm on the other end, she's curled up, I'm curled up, and we only have one blanket. It's not a blanket, but a couch throw; not very thick, and won't completely cover up both of us. Forgot to get a blanket before I shut that door too! So now I am stuck with a decorative pillow and a couch throw, while my husband is snoring in our bed with the four-inch thick micro foam topper, down comforter, and the whole bed to himself. *Dang music man!*

So I do the best I can with what I do not have, and try to settle down for at least the rest of the night's sleep. Maybe! I finally get into my nesting position, cover up the best I can, settle in, and realize that I am as uncomfortable as I've ever been. So I pull the otto-man over to the side of the sofa and stretch my legs out on it. That is a little better for me, and the dog has a little more room. And in the distance I can hear the concert going on in the bedroom.

I finally get to sleep, and guess who has to get up to do his nightly bathroom visit, and it ain't me! The toilet flushes; the squeaky bedroom doors opens, and guess who has come to check on his wife? *Bless his heart!*

"Did you not notice that you had the whole bed to yourself and the elbowing in the ribs had stopped?"

"No! Was I snoring?"

"Yes, hon, now go back to bed."

I was thinking "I really don't want to talk to you right now, and discuss our situation at 3am, now take your anal behind back to bed!"

He then makes an about face, goes back into the bedroom, and does not shut the door behind him. Does he really think I'm going to follow him? In a few minutes, and mind you I haven't gotten back to sleep yet, the concert begins again!

Like Scarlett said, "Tomorrow is another day!" and another opportunity for me to try to get some sleep. I might try to sneak a nap in the afternoon, but every-day without fail, as soon as I close my eyes, I bet you can guess? My husband calls to see what I am doing and why am I taking a nap? Maybe he'll figure it out the next time we try to sleep at night and the bed-room door gets locked, and I'm in but he's not. You think he'll find the sofa as comfortable as I did not? Well, shucks hon, I think he should try it and see!

Nighty night, ya'll, and buy a set of earplugs! Good ones, and must use your husband's credit card too. Maybe buy two pair: one for you and one for the dog. Or trade your husband in for another canine; they don't snore nearly as loud.

WHO LEFT *the* TOILET SEAT UP AGAIN?

And you ladies can go ahead and laugh, but you know exactly what I'm talking about. Heck, the whole dang world knows what I'm talking about. The famous toilet seat that men lift up, but can't for the life of them figure out how to put it down. Every man that I know has failed to pass "Toilet Seat Lowering 101," and I mean this with all of my little pea-picking heart. And anybody out there that begs to differ is a dang storyteller, in my opinion or has never been to the toilet after a man.

When little boys are potty trained, I don't think it's usually the fathers that do that. And I may be wrong about that! I think it's the mothers that start it, and then the fathers chime in and help with it, unless they are a stay at home dad! I thought that as the mother of a little boy, we started with the potty and then graduated to the *big boy* toilet. Somewhere in between I'm wondering if we forgot the step of the toilet seat lowering, and this has been ingrained in them for so long that they just can't relearn the process.

Lift up, do your duty, put down! Lift up, put down! *What in the heck is so difficult about that*? If they can learn to put a lid back on a Tupperware container, they can learn to put a lid back down on the toilet.(But they haven't mastered this task either, so who am I kidding?) I can't for the life of me understand why the majority of men leave it up? Don't they realize that someone other than the male species is going to have to come in after them and have to use the same place? And wouldn't it be polite if they would just put the seat down?

If they remember to wash their hands after they do their duty, I dang sure hope so, why can't they put the toilet seat down? It's as simple as ABC! How did they ever get through school, graduate, get a job, get married, raise a family, and still manage to not put the toilet seat down? I really think it is a brain infarct in that part for just plain ole common sense, but then again I am talking about men! Ah hah, I see where I'm heading with this. And they are the wrong sex for good ole common sense, so that may explain a lot. And I'll apologize for saying that, and I should *shut my mouth*, but this is important.

Do you know why it irritates me half to death to go behind a man, especially in my household, and the toilet seat is left up? Let's just say that I have had a few cold, wet experiences or two in the middle of the night, if you get my drift. You know when you get up in the middle of the night half asleep and go to the bathroom and you expect *all* of the toilet to be there. *Are you following me*? And you get into position, lower yourself gently, and you hit the water with a tremendous thud? Now do you get my drift? And now do you feel my pain or wet experience or whatever you want to call it.

This surprise, or rather *"midnight shocker,"* is enough to totally wake you up and forever keep you from going back to sleep. Your tush is wet, your floor is wet, your pajamas are wet, and the only thing that isn't wet in the immediate area is the huge snoring person that left the seat up. Nice and dry, wrapped up in his blanket all snug, and he doesn't have a clue. Not until you get up, turn on the light, and scream at him at the top of your sweet Southern lungs. "Are you crazy? Do you know that you didn't put the toilet seat down, and now I've sat in the water?"

"Huh!" He then rolls right back over and back to making his sweet musical snoring music. *Dang toilet terrorizer!* And he hasn't heard a word that I have said.

I know I shouldn't get so upset about a toilet lid/seat/whatever you want to call it being left up, but I have been tired of it my whole life. It just makes extra work for us women. If I knew men couldn't remember or hated to put it down that much, I would have just cut a hole in the floor and let them have at it. No lift up, no put down, just point and aim! Case closed and no one to upset. *Now wouldn't that be hysterical!*

I've started with this, and I can't quit now. The hole could be cut in the floor, but it would have to have a door of some kind to close it so the critters couldn't get in the house. Critters meaning flies, mosquitoes, nest building birds, you know what I'm talking about. And I know I'm totally getting out of hand with this, but if you wanted to get back at the man or men in your life, just wait until dark, go close the door, and hope they have to get up at some point and go do their duty. Door closed, they don't know it, back splash, and it ain't on the floor! Bingo! Now who is wet, and you're fast asleep or wide-awake and enjoying every minute of it? Ah, hah! Sweet!

The more this story evolves the more wicked I become of finding ways to get back at our inconsiderate male counterparts. It's not that I do this on a daily basis, but it does greet me every day. *And I mean every day*! And I know my husband can hear the loud clang of the seat when I put it down with a mighty force. In my mind I think he does, so I keep banging it just to release some stress. Or I imagine it is his head that I am banging between that and the rim, and I keep banging to my hearts delight.

Ladies, I think this is a habit that we are going to have to live with till death do us part or unless we run them off. So let's just make the best of it! You can't retrain this gender, and there ain't no use in hollering about it, 'cause they never listen to that. Hollering falls on deaf ears, and I am an expert at that! My husband and my son have been deaf for a long time, and proud of it.

So, pick your battles and pick which toilet you use. If you don't want the men in your household to use it, just install a television in the other bathroom and put the remote where they can see it. If you can get a dog with a bone, you can train a man with a TV and a remote. Now that's my analogy and I'm sticking to it!

DON'T YOU JUST LOVE GOING TO *the* "HINEY-COLOGIST"?

Don't even pretend that you don't have any earthly idea what I am talking about, 'cause I know you do! This is the most dreaded thing that you have to do every year, besides getting your teeth cleaned or having your upper lip waxed. Pardon me if you're sensitive about such things! But I don't have a sensitive bone in my body (and that's a big ole fib), so I guess that's why I can talk about and make fun of everything. And LORD knows you should know what a "hiney" is; and just add "expert in the mutilation of" to it, and there you go! Figure it out!

You know exactly what I mean here! That dreaded dang appointment that you have to make, that takes you forever due to a slip of the mind, and when you finally get the number it is busy or you roll over to an automatic answering system. *Don't you just hate that?* You're finally getting around to making that appointment, and you can't even talk to a live person most of the time. "Just leave your name, number, and the time that you called, and we'll get back to you shortly or the next business day." I just bet they will!

So, you finally get the phone call back from a live

person, and they finally set you up for an appointment. I usually prefer an early morning appointment so I can go ahead and get it over with, plus I weigh less. And have just taken a shower and I feel nice and fresh. I won't go there with anymore information, but no Southern woman likes to feel unfresh, so no afternoon appointment will do for me, especially if I have had to work all day.

The day finally arrives, and I have to anticipate that *today's the day!* I have to go, and there ain't no getting around it. It's my duty as a woman, or is it, and it's for my health, so I'll look at it that way, but either way that I look at it does not make me love it any better! I hate it, can't stand it, get stressed over it, anticipate it, and just dang sure don't want to do it! But I've made the appointment, I'm locked in against my will, so I guess I will go!

I get in the car and drive to my morning appointment that I absolutely made sure the receptionist gave me. I've had my shower, I am fresh, and here I come. Not by choice, mind you, but I'm not that unreasonable. *But I can be if pushed!*

I arrive on time, like I always do, sign my name on their little board and have a seat. But first I had to choose if I wanted to sit in the adult section, the well child section, or the sick child section. Choices, choices. They certainly don't have a special section for *"hiney check ups,"* so I guess I'll sit in the adult section.

I sit and wait, sit and wait for about forty-five minutes and three magazines flip-throughs later; I get a call to come to the back. Good thing they had some good magazines to look at or I would have been one irritable gal; probably not anymore irritable than I usually am. Doctors are always late, bless their hearts, but mine is a talker, so it's understandable. Or he's up to his eyeballs in "hineys," but we won't go there.

The office nurses asks me to first stop at the rest room and give her a "*specimen.*" Okay, I can handle that. So I oblige her, and fill the cup to the top, put it in the little trap door, wash, and flush. Checked out all the magazines in there too and the pretty little air fresheners, probably could have stayed awhile in there, but the nurse seemed to want to finish me in a hurry. "Ms. Dowling, are you OK in there?" I thought to myself, "Sure am, if you would just leave me alone, and let me finish getting my decorating tips and recipes in here. Shouldn't have all these nice magazines, unless you're entertaining." So out of the bathroom I went.

She then motioned for me to come into one of those little rooms, which only has an exam table, a stool, and a sink in it. So aesthetic looking, sterile, hard, cold, you know what I mean. She then asked me to take off everything and put on one of those little paper gowns and keep it open in the front. She then gave me a sheet, and told me she would be back in a minute. *Yeah, I bet!* Oh, the stress begins.

Why can they not give you a cotton flannel gown that opens in front? Why this recycled paper thang? It scratches and ain't a bit comfortable. And I never can figure out where the front is, always get it on backwards first; and covering up the rest of me with that starched, white itchy sheet. Didn't put any Downy in the rinse water when they laundered these things, if you do happen to get a real cloth one. Heck, it might be paper too, and you're just out of luck with finding anything soft.

The nurse had already laid out that plastic "hiney" speculum, the KY jelly, and those little bitty scrapers. I already began hating the thought of all of this. You feel like they are fixing to dissect you, and are turning you inside out and upside down. Do you think I can escape now, or if they'd even notice if I left everything and ran! Probably so! Don't think it hasn't crossed my mind and my hand is on the door.

Okay, come back to my senses, I get undressed and put on this cold paper gown and got my cold white sheet and pulled it over me and got onto the table. The cold slab of a table, mind you! And dang it, it had paper on it too. This office is responsible for killing a lot of trees in a short time. And why is it so cold in here? Can't they afford heat in here, for what we're paying them for all this abuse? They could have gotten a heated table too! But a nice soft thermal blanket in pink would have been even nicer. In my dreams!

Well, the good doctor comes in and gives me a grin. Nice doctor, nice person, don't know why he's grinning. He isn't fixing to get turned inside out! I am, and not liking it one bit. Oh well, I'll just grin and *not* bear it, and it will be over in just a minute or two. That is unless he starts talking to me or his nurse, answers a page, picks up the phone, etc.

I won't go into detail about the next two happenings, but I can tell you that it wasn't and never is pleasant. It depends on where they go to medical school. And this group never warmed anything. Its liking sticking your hands in ice and putting them on your butt! *Brr*! Plus I don't like having to put my cold feet in those metal, ice cold, insensitive, not godly stirrups. I ain't fixing to ride no horse, so I don't see the point of those things.

Plus, I don't like the doctor to get into a place where I can't see him. I have worked in a doctor's office, and I know what goes on when the patient is out of eye-shot of the doctor, and they would not be amused. Another story though!

I did survive this, but I wasn't happy about it. Just glad that it was over, and that it would be 365 days before I graced these doors and subjected my *"parts"* to ice cold metal and freezing temperatures for a while. I wonder if the doctors, and most of the "hiney-colo-gists" I know are male, would like to be subjected to this kind of abuse. I realize it is not abuse, but ask them to strip naked, give them a couple of pieces of paper, and ask them to lie down on anything that is thirty-two degrees or below. Bet they'd change their tune and opt for flannel and a heating pad.

So gals, you and I are in this together! We have to do this, so we might as well make fun of it as we go along. Lord knows it ain't gonna get any better! But if it does, I'll be the first to let you know. But on the other hand, if it gets any worse, I'll be screaming from the top of my lungs, and you'll hear me too! Then instead of writing, I might be trying to invent a hand warmer for them doctors and a mirror so that I can see every move and every face they make.

Can't pull anything over on me, ya'll, and that's a fact, unless it's one of those dang itchy paper sheets. *Ouch!*

NOW *the* REST *of the* STORY ... WE'RE NOT DONE YET!

Sorry girls, and maybe a guy or two that dares to read this, I don't think the above story would be complete without a conversation or two about the good ole mammogram! At the office, we call it *"getting our anatomies squeezed."* You know exactly what anatomy I am squawking about! This is very comparable to the above story in the rules of torture, and it would be a big toss up to see which one is worse! *Care to flip a coin?*

I wonder who in the heck designed the mammogram machine? I would like to just kick their big fat tush! Or put their big fat tush in there, and give it a big ole squeeze and let them hold on for dear life. Might go take a lunch, go to the potty, and read a magazine or talk on the phone for about 20–30 minutes, and then go back and check on them. See if they're still holding on! *I should shut my mouth!*

I really wouldn't put them in there unwillingly, 'cause that would be mean! Would tickle the heck out of me though! Wicked aren't I, but I do like to give someone or something that causes me any kind pain or discomfort, just a little bit of their own torture. I don't think that is un-Christian like. Doesn't it say in the Bible *"an eye for an eye"*? Well, my interpretation is a tush for a…and I ain't even going there, but you get the picture.

Oh well, getting back to the dang mammogram that I am dreading to have along with my annual "hiney" exam. I have to have an appointment for this too! *Dern it*! So I call the number that I have been given by my doctor's office, and it is also a recording. What the heck, are they too cheap to hire real people anymore? Push one, then ya, ya, ya, push two, ya, ya, ya, leave your name and number and we will call you back shortly. Now where have I heard this junk before?

Cutting to the chase, I finally got my appointment. *Good for me!* Another tortuous appointment coming up, and I will have to stress out again. This torture chamber won't come up for at least a month, so I have got time. With a machine that can scan a woman every fifteen minutes, I don't understand why it takes so long to get in there. Surely there aren't that many women wanting to be tortured at one time, but I guess there are.

Well, my month went by quickly, and my appointment time and the day arrived. Dang it, I would rather have a tooth pulled. 'Cause that machine feels like it is going to pull both of my anatomies off.

You know I'm not lying, you've done it, now say it ain't so! If you say it doesn't feel like that, then you must have been very drugged up or slid out of the thing. *It hurts*! No two ways about it. I don't mean to sound so crude, but it's the only way that I can describe it.

I finally arrived at my appointment, walked in, and

signed their little board. I didn't have to wait but about five-ten minutes, bless them, and my sweet friend Lora came out to get me. You see, she is a sweetheart, and has been torturing me for three years, and every year I come back. If she weren't so sweet and dear, I would smack her, but she's just doing her job. And she does it well, while I'm hanging on for dear life.

You just can't make a mammogram comfortable. *There just ain't no way in heck!* But I guess it has to be done, it is very important, and it does help to save lives. I'll just keep telling myself that, over and over and over, while I am slowly walking toward the torture chamber.

Lora walked me down the hall to a little room, and here we go again. She gave me a gown, and it was a cloth one thank goodness, and she wanted me to open it in the front. That's okay; at least it wasn't ice cold and scratchy, maybe a touch of Downy in the material. So I can't kick and scream too much, but maybe just a little for effect.

So like a good person that I can be, I put the little gown on, wiped the residue of my deodorant off, took my jewelry off, and was ready for the chamber. I walked out and Lora asked me to stand right here, put one of my anatomies on a cold, plastic slab, and came at it from the other side with a sliding piece of even colder plastic. Tight, tight, tight, and I wondered if she was ever going to stop. "Hold your breath," Lora said, and I almost replied, "How can I not?" When something is squeezing the life out of you, your last thought is to breathe, maybe to scream, but certainly not to breathe. And if you start seeing stars from lack of oxygen, I guess you're doing exactly what she told you to do!

Sounded like soft shooting sounds, then, "Ok, you can relax now." Ha! Not while this thing still has my anatomy! Release me, please, from its bondage. Lora did and I gave a big sigh of relief, made a face, and then geared up for round two. That didn't go any better, but within a minute or two it was all over. *Thank goodness in Heaven!*

I looked down, and I am exaggerating here just a bit, but instead of round anatomies, they seemed to be taking on an elliptical shape. *No dang wonder!* They just about went through a cookie press, and they aren't supposed to do that. They were trying to go through it, but the rest of me wasn't.

Lora smiled sweetly at me like she always does and apologized to the hilt. She didn't have to do that, I knew what I was in for, and she does a good job at torturing me! She told me to put my clothes back on and that I was finished. You dang tootin'; for 365 more days!

I finished getting dressed, gave Lora a hug, and made a quiet exit out of the building. I was through with everything for one year, so I might as well go celebrate. But I'm too sore and cranky now, so I guess I'll save that for another time.

But a little pitiful pout and a *"poor me"* written all over my face when my husband comes home might not hurt. Might even get him to cook or take me out to dinner for all of my suffering. But if he heads to the television or the bathroom as soon as he gets home, my efforts will be in vane, or I'll have to hold that face for a long time. Nah, might as well just order take out and let him pay for it.

Girls, I still have his credit card, you know!

WHY IS THERE NEVER ANY TOILET PAPER IN *the* BATHROOM?

I can't for the life of me understand why my wonderful family can't remember to put any toilet paper in the bathroom. They must be the last person to go in there, 'cause I know it ain't me. They always finish the roll, leave the cardboard holder, and walk out without pulling it off and putting a fresh roll on it for the next person. That's too much brain activity for them, so I guess this is why they never do it!

Changing the roll of toilet paper has to be the easiest no-brainer that there is. You could train a monkey to do it, but you can't train my family. They will literally stack the new roll on top of an empty cardboard holder to keep from having to change the roll. But if there's no paper in the bathroom, they will just walk out and think the paper is going to walk in there by themselves. Lazy, lazy, lazy … that's what I have to say about that. Or rather they know that they've done it and just want to tick me off! But why is this any different from some of the other things that I have already told you about?

I hate it when I go in the bathroom and find no toilet paper. Irritates the heck out of me, and then I have to go searching. They probably have used up all of the extra rolls, and the large packages of toilet paper are downstairs in the shop. And guess who is going to have to put their shoes on, possibly get dressed and go downstairs to get it? *Well it ain't them!* That's way too much thinking and totally out of their league.

So I put my shoes on, go downstairs to the shop, and grab one of those large plastic-wrapped packages that have "toilet paper" written on it. It has twelve rolls, so that should cover my lazy family and me for a long time. It better cover me, and I'm not really worried about them at this point, and I think I might just hide some of the rolls for a future *"no paper in here"* day!

I then go around to every bathroom and put several rolls in baskets, under the sink or in the *drawers*, so when nature calls, there will be adequate supplies. Don't want anyone to go lacking, if you know what I mean. So I'll be a good wife and momma and make sure they have what they need. I'm trying to convince myself that this is the right thing to do, even though the anticipation of an empty toilet roll holder, which will eventually greet me, creeps into my mind.

But wouldn't it be rebellious of me if the next time they didn't replace the toilet paper roll or go down and get more, that I just sat there in my comfy chair when they decided to take a little trip in there. I think they might realize in a hurry that there was no paper and start yelling for help.

I should just let them yell, think about them *"dripping dry"* or whatever, and enjoy the music of their distress. I would probably act like I wasn't here and listen to them continue to yell. Might just go outside and take a walk around the block and listen to the pretty sounds of outdoors, while they still sit unwillingly, perched on their throne. I do feel their pain, but I am going to let them sit for as long as I think they should, and it might be a long time.

Slowly but surely, I would decide to feel sorry for the poor unfortunate soul that is sitting in the bathroom with no paper. The yelling has stopped, but now I hear, "Come on, bring me some paper!" So I give in. No, not yet. I decide to throw in an empty cardboard holder, for a little more of a poke in the ribs and a great big hint: Change the freaking roll!

Another yell and I can't write it here, but I think I have made my point. Oh yeah, I think I have made it very well. Ha ... this is funnier than a three-ring circus, and I am totally in control. And I am the only one laughing. Bless the throne-sitters heart!

Well, my victim finally comes out, and there is a glare in their eyes.

"That wasn't funny!"

"I thought it was absolutely hilarious, and now do you get my drift?"

More glaring, pouting, and silence. *I guess not!* And my plot was all for nothing. Not sure if they learned anything here. I guess we'll see with the next change of the roll.

Update ... my family is still not putting toilet paper in the bathroom, but they will go and get it when it runs completely out. *That is kinda scary, don't you think!* At least, they might be thinking about it a little bit. I guess they are tired of "drip-drying" or whatever, and I haven't been home to rescue anybody in a long time, or either I have just tuned them out. I think it might be the later. I haven't heard anybody scream or fall on the floor with their undies around their ankles because they were looking for a roll. I know...too much information! Oh well, if you know me personally, you know I'm uninhibited as heck, and I'll say anything.

But I only tell the truth, though I might stretch it a bit here and there! Now that *is* the truth, ya'll!

ME... COLOR MY HAIR
...ABSOLUTELY!

Don't you just love it when you reach the age that you have to use hair color, forever and ever amen! Or just let your hair go au naturale, age about ten years, and start getting downright mean with everyone. It's amazing what a little $6.99 box of hair color can prevent.

Please don't get me wrong! I think gray hair is very attractive on a lot of women, maybe more so than their natural color. I have some friends and family that look absolutely fabulous with silver locks, and they have never looked better. But I am scared to death that I won't be as lucky, and look absolutely dreadful, so I am trying to put the reins on Mother Nature, or at least cover her up until I'm good and ready! I guess I haven't let the full canvas come to life, 'cause every time I start seeing the gray roots showing, I run for the drug store and aisle 2.

When I reached my teenage years, I couldn't wait to put some of that stuff called Sun-In on my hair. Wanted to be a blonde! That's all I could think about, because I did think blondes had more fun. I started out with full strength peroxide on my hair, which lightened it a bit, lemon juice, vinegar, anything that my friends suggested. After this didn't work too well, I retaliated and went for the Sun-In!

Well, I bought it, sprayed it on my hair, and went out in the sun to make my blonde visions appear. I waited, sprayed some more, and waited; no blonde! What I got was brilliant red hair without a streak of blonde in it! Most of my friends tried it too, and they got the same No blonde results. You see, I forgot to mention that we were all brunettes, and peroxide and brunette don't produce blonde.

After this episode, we all had to let our hair grow out, dark roots and all, since back in the day young teenage girls didn't dye their hair, only put stuff on it to turn it another color. So we all had to suffer with the roots until our hair grew out. Winter red hair and dark roots, yuck!

When I became an adult, I must not have learned a lesson from that Sun-In episode, so I decided to do it again. Wanted to be the blond that I knew I couldn't be! *Again!* So I started putting hair color on it in blond shades, so guess what? I got red hair again.

Ah…but one time I remember that I didn't like the shade of red that it had become, so I went and bought another color to try to get it back to my natural color. Well, sometimes when you buy hair color, the color is says on the box is not necessarily the color that you will end up with. *Fancy that!* I put this color on after I got it home and ended up looking like I was from the Far East. Nothing wrong with that, but that is not my natural color, jet black. So, with a scarf on my head, I went back to the store.

Not thinking, and I am well known for not always

doing that, I got a color stripper to put on my hair, hopefully just to take the color off. Well, I put it on, waited a while, and my hair, to my horror, turned snow white. Uh oh...I had really messed up!

The scarf when back on my head, and it was back to the store again, this time to buy my correct shade, but maybe a little lighter; not blond and not black. I just hoped that my flip a coin of the hair color would land me on my correct shade. Didn't want to look like a stripper (*no pun intended*) and didn't want to look like a mafia boss's wife either! And the way the cashier at the drug store was snickering when she looked my way, you woulda thought she knew what I had been up to. And I bet she did! "Another idiot trying to dye her hair the wrong color!"

This time I went back home and put yet another shade of light ash brown on my hair, and finally the color looked sorta like it should. But it was "frizzed to high heaven," like my Nanny would have said. My hair was frizzy, dry, and looked like something out of the 60's hippie movement, and what was I going to do now? I just hoped that all of it wouldn't break until I could give it a hot oil treatment.

Luckily for me, my hair was able to survive with a lot of conditioner and more conditioner, some hot oil treatments, and more conditioner. My hair stylist was appalled by what *garbage* I had put on my hair, and it was a wonder that it didn't all fall out. Lesson learned, at least for the moment!

Well, I left the hair color alone for most of my twenties and thirties, until those first little glorious grays started to appear, and I was tired of pulling them out! Literally, I would yank them out one by one, until I couldn't see them anymore. But they would just change positions on my head and keep coming back. Plus, I was afraid that I was going to put bald spots in my head from all the yanking.

When it came time to make a decision about the hair color, I remembered my past experiences and decided just to try a hair stain or semi permanent that would only last for about twenty washings. That way if I really screwed it up, it wouldn't be permanent. But I had to find a color that wouldn't be too dark, and that was the hard part.

I have some pictures of my skin and me in which my hair looks jet black, and my skin is so white that I might look a little gothic. Just kidding, but not really, my hair was a little dark. But gradually, all of the colors, or stains, permanent, or semi-permanent always fade, and you are always left with one thing: gray hair!

So get used to it, honey, if you don't like gray hair, you will be coloring it for the rest of your life. You can do it yourself and risk looking gothic, or pay through the nose and let a professional do it! Either way, if you don't keep it up, you will have gray hair. Unless you are lucky enough to have been born with the good genes that don't give you the grays. But unfortunately, I come from a long time of silver haired ladies and bald men. So if I have to flip a coin, as to which I'd rather be, it won't be bald.

I think I have mastered the hair color guessing game, and now just do it myself with one brand and one color. On occasion I'll let a professional do it when I want a little pampering. Nothing wrong with that, all of us middle-aged gals love to be pampered and we deserve it! We'll probably add a facial and a massage when we go for that hair coloring too! *Cause we deserve it!* Plus if we have our husband's credit card, we don't mind a bit.

I guess when I get older, and more mature (never!), I might quit all of this vanity and let my hair grow out gray, like nature intended. But nature also intended me to have hairy legs and underarms (don't provide razors), no makeup (don't provide Ms. Lauder), and plain nails (no Opi here!). So I'll just have to give nature a *"butt-whooping"* and do things my way, at least for a little while longer.

So here's to hair color and all of its wonderful boosts of self-esteem and glamour that it gives to us all! Ain't no true Southern gal ever denied herself a little glamour! Or a Northern, Western, Mid-Western, etc. gal either.

Happy coloring, ya'll! But just be sure to hide the box!

LITTLE SOUTHERN BELLES, BEAUTY PAGEANTS, *and* CAT FIGHTS

When my daughter Kelli was in grammar, middle, and high school, she was in several beauty pageants. Beauty pageants in a very little *podunk* town, and I mean little. They called the area Mid Valley or the "valley" for short, and you would have thought she was in the Miss America pageant by the stuff that went on in these pageants.

I was born and raised to be polite, have manners, and try not to be unkind to anyone. I was also taught in church not to be jealous or envious, not to covet thy neighbor, and just plain not to be unkind. "Do unto others as you would have them do unto you" is what I grew up with. That is until you put your daughter in a beauty pageant and realize that nobody else abides by that rule, and you just come short of a *catfight*!

Let's back up a minute and tell you what's involved in the preliminaries to a "Podunk USA" kiddie pageant. In grammar school, it is casual wear and semi-evening wear. Hair and light makeup must be done, new shoes, etc. Not too much of a big deal!

In middle school, it is casual wear, talent costume,

and eveningwear. We have to have a "big girl" hair-style, heavy makeup, new shoes x 2, and a *killer* evening dress in white. We spend many hours on our talent, which is a jazz dance, but we have never taken jazz in our life. We have to go to the formal wear store in the downtown area and select a dress, which costs about $200, but then we manage to borrow one from a friend. Still not too much of a big deal!

In high school, it becomes a whole lot more involved. We have to have group routine wear, casual wear, talent wear, and a killer evening dress. We spend several weeks in preparation for this pageant, several hours of training for our clogging talent, and several hours of trying to mentally prepare for all of this. We go back to the formal wear store, select a dress, which costs a month's mortgage. We go back for more heavy makeup, the right hairstyle, acrylic manicured nails, etc; a lot more involvement with this one.

Oh … and let's don't forget the photo portfolio that cost a half month's mortgage so that we could present this before the pageant. *Gotta look good*! Had to have more hair styling and makeup before we had this done too! Plus several new outfits! Geez!

Whew … have you had enough preparation tips? The ones just mentioned were only the school pageants that she was involved in. That doesn't include the community pageants that she was also in, and the Little Miss This and That that she entered. All of them requiring, oh yes, entrance fees, more dresses, more makeup, and more hair styling! I must have been a *"hair brain"* to allow her to be in all of these.

Kelli won a lot of them that she entered, and lost some of them too. I guess the bug hit her, when she won the first one she was ever in: Little Miss 6th Grade. Then it was Little Miss 7th Grade. Pageant after pageant she would win, or be first or second runner up. To hear some of these mothers talk about these pageants, you would think it was Miss America.

Well, as I said, I was raised to be polite. Heck...I enjoyed these pageants, but didn't really take it too seriously. They are just kids, these are for fun, helping these little girls to become ladies,etc. I certainly didn't want her or me to get in a fight over it! But I bet you five dollars, that a lot of those other contestants and mommas would have *"scrapped"* in a minute!

The first pageant Kelli was in, everything was fine. Congratulations from her friends and some of the other mothers. I really didn't hear an unkind word. The second one, one of the kid's said, "She always wins," and snotted off with her mother in tow. Neither one of them congratulated Kelli! But this was just the beginning.

Another pageant that she was in, one of the girls that she had beat in a previous pageant offered to walk with her before it got started. I had always tried not to hover too much over Kelli in the dressing room before hand, so if she didn't need me to help her dress, I would excuse myself. But on this occasion, Kelli had caught the bottom of her dress in her zipper so that the back of her dress was riding up, and her underwear was showing. The other girl could plainly see this, but never bothered to tell her. Someone else told her when the pageant was just about to start. *Little Miss Snotty Darling*, I said to myself.

Not very nice, but I do tend to get my feathers ruffled when someone mistreats my children. That Little

Miss Snotty Darling won the pageant that night, and I made sure that Kelli congratulated her.

Another time, this same Little Miss Snotty Darling was in another pageant with my daughter, and it was just the two of them together. Well, this time Kelli won, and you should have seen the look on Little Miss Snotty Darling's face! If she had been in a field of cow pilings, her face wouldn't have been any different. *Shut my mouth!*

This time her momma was not very friendly to me; almost the "constipated look" that she shot my way. I just smiled in my sweet Southern way, and said how nice her Little Miss Snotty Darling looked. I could feel the claws coming out, but that wouldn't have been very nice.

A few years later, which was to be Kelli's last pageant, Little Miss Snotty Darling was there again. She and my daughter had had several *"head to heads"* over the years involving boyfriends, pageant results, you said-I said episodes, phone calls to me from her lying (oops!) momma, etc. I had had enough of Little Miss Snotty Darling by this time.

During this pageant, the girls were asked to walk across the stage, while an emcee read many interesting things about the young lady. Things such as where they wanted to go to college, hobbies, what they did in their spare time, etc. Well, I forgot to mention that my then ten-year-old son just happened to be there, and other than fighting with his sister most of the time, was actually quite protective of her.

Little Miss Snotty Darling's turn to parade across the stage came up, and prance away she did. When they got to the part where they said that "she likes to spend time with her friends," well my little son, as unquiet as he is, blasted out as loud as you could possibly be: "She doesn't have any friends!" So the whole auditorium heard it, including Little Miss Snotty Darling's mother.

Well, I was sitting a few rows up from her momma, and there was no place to hide. Not that I really wanted to, 'cause Little Miss Snotty Darling deserved it, and I couldn't resist letting that woman see the look on my face. Hee hee, now ain't that mean? But I gave her the look of, "Oh my, I am so sorry." But all the while I was hysterically laughing so hard on the inside that I almost *peed* in my pants. Good thing the ladies room was nearby!

Little Miss Snotty Darling didn't win this one, thank the LORD, but one of Kelli's good friends, and what a fine winner she was. Kelli came in as 2nd runner up, and we were all very proud of her. After the pageant, I don't think Little Miss Snotty Darling congratulated anyone, just huffed and puffed and with her momma in tow, left the building. Never saw the girl smile again after that! Her momma didn't either.

I don't know why people, or rather parents, get so serious over these things. Some of these little girls, or rather the ones that I had the treachery of being in their company, were spoiled little snotty-nosed brats! A lot of them talked to their mommas just awful. If that were my momma, she would have not hesitated to lay the law down and would have taken my pretty pageant butt right home. Ain't no sense in kids being so sassy to their parents. I was never allowed to get away with it! (That current child abuse thing comes to mind!)

So if you decide to put your little darling in a beauty pageant, take caution. Sometimes they aren't what you expected. A lot of competition, stressed out kids and parents, and you'll have a lot of dust collecting trophies to remember the glorious event by. Later on, you will shove those trophies in a box, beg the kid to take them, and they will end up in a dumpster like my daughter's did, minus the two dollar face plate. All this so you could say that *your* darling was in a beauty pageant. And it only cost you about $1000 a pageant to be able to say it! And that's before they finish high school.

Nah...I wouldn't have missed it either, part of growing up and having my own exceptional, snot-nose brat. Wouldn't have missed giving the evil eye to Little Miss Snotty Darling's momma either, but I really wanted to swat her and her daughter with my pocketbook. Not a very ladylike thing to say, huh? But who says I have to be a lady all of the time. *Wanna scrap?*

Now I should *shut my mouth* on that one, but I won't!

Hee hee, can't wait till I have a granddaughter!

WHY I PREFER BEING FRIENDS WITH MEN OVER WOMEN ... MOST *of the* TIME!

Now, don't get your fanny feathers ruffled, girls! I did say most of the time, not all of the time. But my daughter and I are on the same page with this one, so I guess we have a lot of explaining to do, or rather some defending to do after all the sassy things we have said about men so far! Heck, this is just part of the fun, so here goes.

I do love all of the women friends in my life, every one of them. I have several close friendships with women, and we share just about everything. But being a close friend with a man is just a lot different than being friends with a woman. And I will give you several reasons why:

1) Women tend to be competitive with other women, men don't!

Now don't lie, girls, but when your good friend has a prettier outfit on than you do, you do get a little envious. You look her up and down from head to toe, check out her shoes, her pants/skirt, top/blouse, hairdo, makeup, fine lines and wrinkles, and her jewelry. Probably her nails, teeth whiteness, whether she has roots or not, etc. Now don't lie, most of us, and I say us, tend to do that! *Yes we do!*

I love to watch women when they greet each other. Just like clockwork! Ha! *I'm right, aren't I?* Observe the next time that you strike up a close conversation with another female and they are in your space; just watch!

I have a relative that every time she sees me she looks me up and down and will find something to try to impress me with. "I've lost ten pounds, I got a new diamond, I've redecorated my house," or she'll say some other nonsense. She does it every time, just like clockwork. I guess she finds some sort of thing that I have that she doesn't, so she makes up things to help fight her insecurity or whatever her problem is at the moment. Now argue with me that women aren't competitive. *You know I'm right, girlfriend!*

Men, on the other hand, could care less what you have on, at least below the waist. Granted they might look at your eyes, and at maybe some of your God given assets, but definitely not your shoes, your jewelry, or your new designer purse. Ha! If they do, they are definitely a *girlfriend*, if you know what I mean?

Men are not in competition with you, at least not on a friendship level. They don't care if you have more expensive designer jeans than they do, your jewelry is better than theirs, or if you have it a little better than they do. Or at least they don't talk about it!

All of my men friends are in it for the total friendship of it. We laugh, we talk a lot, we share opinions and frustrations, we have gripe sessions, we disagree, but it is all in a friendly manner. We are in it for the friendship, and because we don't have to worry about having competition between us. *'Cause it ain't about that!*

Plus, you can actually talk to one of your men friends, probably a little more frank than you can talk to your spouse. And you can probably be more open and honest, because your spouse might think you're crazy, and your men friends will know you are. You can be totally yourself, good or bad, with your men friends, and they don't care if you make a fool of yourself. They'll even help you get home. Your spouse, on the other hand, won't allow you to act that way and will definitely take you home!

2) Two women might have a hard time living together; a man and a woman living together platonically would probably get along well.

My daughter found this out very quickly in college. She had many women roommates and didn't get along with any of them. "But Mom, I just don't get along with girls, I want a guy for a roommate." And I guess I couldn't argue with her there.

The first girl she roomed with shared her side of the room with her boyfriend. She used her dishes/bowls to have a hangover in. And some of her other roommates ate all of her food and didn't replace it. All of her college life I heard complaints about her roommates. So in turn, having being fed up with all of her girl roommates, she would spend most of her time with her guy friends. At least they cooked for her and fed her. Do you think that any of her girlfriends would have done that for her? *Heck fire no!*

3) Women can be more at ease with a male friend than they can other women.

I'll have to use my friend John as an example. When

we get together, our friendship and total respect for one another puts us both at ease so much that we don't have to feel uncomfortable. He is a wonderful friend and one that I look forward to seeing and spending time with. We don't have to try to impress each other ever. And we have been great friends for years, and I consider him one of my very best friends.

If I get together with a bunch of women, and it does depend on the group that I'm with, I sometimes feel the stress before I ever get there. *And don't say that you've never felt that way!* When you're with a group of women, I don't know what it is, but I feel uneasy some of the time. It takes me a while to warm up! I think I worry that I look fat, have gained weight, if my hair is okay, if my clothes look all right, and on and on and on.

With a male friend, I just show up. It might be wrinkled jeans, no makeup, and *bed hair*, if I'm in a hurry. I don't seem to worry about these things, just that I am delighted to be with my friend, not if I look good enough to do the runway! Ha!

4) Women tend to take their frustrations out on other women, especially if they are good friends!

Using my daughter as an example, if she is in a mood or "mid-cycle," so to speak, she usually will snap at me and misinterpret everything that I say. I usually have to not talk during these times or risk having *my head bitten off.* On the other hand, two men also live in this house, but she just smiles at them and doesn't say a word. *So what's up with that?* I definitely have the wrong anatomy for her to be nice to me at this time.

I notice other women that I know will totally be in

a "bad mood," but if a man comes along, the attitude will probably disappear. *What's up with that again?* Women seem to totally change direction if a male friend comes along, but just the opposite for a female. There goes that anatomy thing again!

And in the workplace, if a woman gets promoted over another woman, even if she deserved it, the one that didn't get promoted will stew like a *"sore tail cat,"* like my mom used to say, and they will stay that way for a long time. On the other hand, if a man is chosen, she probably won't stew nearly as long. But she will talk about it for days, longer if the woman had been chosen over her. And talk about her like she's a dog, with claws out, eyes drawn, and a hiss on her lips.

4) Women are more critical of other women.

"Did you see what she had on?" "Why did she say that?" "Did you see her sitting that close to my husband?" "The nerve of her!" "She never calls me." How many times have you heard at least a few of these? But do you ever hear, "Did you see what he had on?" "Why did he say that?" "Did you see him sitting so close to my husband?" "The nerve of him!" Not as much I bet, hon.

In the above statements, if a man sat close to your husband, you wouldn't think a thing of it. *In heavy conversation,* you might think. Not that a man was trying to make a pass at your husband. But you would definitely think it of a woman. But innocently, she might just have a hearing problem and needs to get closer, she is about to fall off the couch, she is sitting next to a person on the other side that is pushing her forward, she only considers your husband a friend, or she is discussing something very confidential like how she can help him pick out a present for you, that she has to sit closer. *Now don't you feel like a dog?* Bow-wow!

Women tend to be more critical of other women, almost like it is a standoff! They tend to be more complimentary of men, almost looking for approval. But not too complimentary of women, since this might make them feel inferior. *Funny thing about anatomy, huh?*

So ask me again why I might prefer being friends with men versus women. Well, I think my defense rests. I'm still trying to figure out why women want to pulverize other women, but I guess it's in the hormones, and the good LORD gave them to us, so it's not for me to question. But if you think about it, in nature, a lot of female-to-female species do not get along either. They even try to kill each other. So I hope we don't get that carried away. *Mercy!*

So if you see me at work, or at the mall, or in my neighborhood talking to a man, don't criticize and make up things about us, because we're just friends! *That's it!* So take your hormones and your opinions and keep it to yourself. I've learned a long time ago to *shut my mouth* about such things and welcome friendships with all types of people; even gripey women!

What other people think doesn't matter anyway! And like my icon Scarlett who said, "Fiddle dee dee," she was exactly right about that! So lighten up, ya'll, and see people for who they are and not what side they zip up their britches on.

I'M MIDDLE-AGED, STILL "GOT IT," SOPHISTICATED *and* MY LIFE'S AMBITION IS TO BE ...A DOG POOPER-SCOOPER!

It was looking at the newspaper the other day, and I almost *wet my pants*! On one of the pages was an ad for a doggie pooper-scooper service. You could hire them however you wanted: daily, weekly, and monthly. Also depended on the size of the yard, the size of the dog, and how much poop they needed to shovel. *How hilarious is that?*

I see a vision, and this is a very exaggerated vision. A bleached blond woman comes out of the pooper-scooper truck, mink coat, and new white Keds on with her pooper-scooper in one hand and a Food Lion bag in the other. And don't forget the J Kennedy sunglasses and the snotty attitude. She spies the pile waiting before her and heads for it with all of her might. Yes...she reaches for it, reaches some more, scoops it up, and puts it in her bag and...touchdown! Another pile has been demolished. *And yes, yes, yes what have I been drinking so early in the morning to be able to envision this?*

I can see my favorite Marilyn-look-alike doing this, and her name will remain anonymous. You know, she is one of those family members that you don't want to tell anyone about. You love her, but you don't dare tell a soul what she does or says. No Carhartt jacket for her to do this type of job in, but her mink coat, because it is warm and she can!

Enough of that! I'm not trying to "dog" these guys that put the ad in the paper, no pun intended, because they just might have something here! Getting to work outside at their own leisure and taking care of what Mother Nature left on the ground. Being out in the sunshine and fresh air, not having to stay in an office, getting to wear jeans or a mink coat if you prefer that, and not having a boss watch every move you make. Sounds better all the time!

I am always trying to find the perfect job, and I have been doing this for most of my working life. Ha! Just ask my husband. "You're just like one of my other friends, changes jobs all the time and doesn't know what he wants to be when he grows up! *Who said anything about growing up?* I haven't grown up yet, so why start now? Then I don't have to make excuses for the stupid stuff that I do or say or write or send or act out or...

I am in the golden decade of my life. Middle age is the *"bomb,"* and if you're smart, you won't beg to differ. I am finally getting to be just me, Kathy, and not somebody's momma, wife, sister, daughter, aunt, etc.; coming first place in the sentence, and I like it just fine. Just me, myself, and I. Ta da! Ain't that selfish, self-centered, rude, mean, snotty, stuck-up, arrogant, and on and on and on. Certainly is, and I'm loving every non-ladylike minute of it. *So bite me if you please!*

Getting back to the pooper-scooper job, it does sound hilarious, but also quite interesting. One of my problems would be if I were somewhere where the topic of your occupation came up, what would I tell people? *Certainly couldn't tell them that!* How about waste diffuser, environmentalist, canine companion, natural specialist, d-d dumper (if they don't ask what the d-d for *doo doo* stands for, you are home free). Or heck, just make up something else, that you're self-employed and you're working for the environment. If some nosey so and so really wants to pry, say you have to excuse yourself and head for the beverages.

I do think that a Southern, middle-aged, fairly good-looking woman with a sense of humor would be a good addition to this poop scooping team. When customers call up, she could answer the phone with a very Southern and sweet accent and say, *"May I help you, puh-lease!"* The person on the line might be surprised to hear a Southern belle on the other end of the line, plus a woman at that. Not some gruff man that answers the phone as, *"Ye-ah, Bubba here, ya need some poop scooped?"*

I think I could bring a little class to this business, that is the dog's *"business,"* and make it not so distasteful for customers to call. Maybe add a little color to the service trucks, nice chic uniforms for the guys and gals so they don't look like the garbage team coming (excuse me, sanitation supervisors), neon-colored pooper scoopers with matching collection bags, and scented receipts for the customers in their choice of savory beef stew, grilled chicken and vegetables, or lamb and rice. And a mink coat for me for special emergencies.

What kind of emergencies? Like a real scooping problem? I could show up in that mink coat, and the customers would be so overwhelmed with laughter and curiosity that they would forget all about whatever problem they had. Plus I would have the blond wig on, the J Kennedy sunglasses, and the new white Keds. Now if that isn't something to throw your fanny and your thoughts out of gear, I don't know what will.

Well, enough making fun of the professional pooper-scoopers. I wasn't really making fun; it just seemed to make a nice little story. I've just never heard of anyone doing that, and I do think it is a much-needed service. Especially for some lazy people in this neighborhood of mine that don't think twice about leaving it for days on their lawn or leaving it on mine. *Shut my mouth!* No, I won't!

There's nothing more disgusting. *E…ew!!*

So here's to the local scoopers! Carry on, ladies and gentlemen, and good luck with your business. I hope you do very well, and if you ever need someone to ride along with you and wear a mink coat, just give my relative that has one a call. 1–800-Marilyn.

Bless her heart!

LEAVE ME ALONE, *and* DON'T DRESS ME LIKE AN OLD LADY!

I guess I could probably turn this around and say, "quit allowing my relative to dress like an old lady!" I won't say who this relative is, 'cause she would absolutely kill me, and I do value my life a little bit. I don't think I dress like an old lady, but she does on occasion, well...maybe sometimes. And I might be exaggerating a little bit here for effect!

This person is a very nice-looking, trim lady to be her age; and she ain't old by no means. But sometimes I think she thinks she is. She talks about death and dying a little bit too much for me, 'cause I'm so busy living and writing that I don't have time for it. I'll let other people worry about that kind of stuff when I am gone. But just to spite everybody, I am not going anywhere for a long time! Live to be a hundred, I will, and I'll have the fanciest wardrobe even then.

Getting back to dressing; I try to get her to upgrade her wardrobe a bit, but she constantly says, "I'm too old to wear that!" *Wear what,* I think to myself? *Stylish clothes?* Cotton and silk, instead of polyester; royal blue and coral, instead of drab brown and olive green; jewelry that sparkles, instead of none. I could go on and on!

Have you ever looked at the name brands of some of these clothes that I wouldn't be caught dead in? Well, so I don't have lawsuits flying around, you will have to guess. The styles are not too bad, just not for me, and all that polyester. And the names are not exactly a winner either for this stage in my life. Anything with the word bag or sag or hag in it is just not right for the middle-aged woman. It might be okay for someone that is in their *"way up yonder years,"* but not for a woman of my age or this nameless relative that I am talking about.

Another one is this catalog that comes around in the mail, and everything is made of polyester, and most of it is pull-on kind of stuff, buy one get one free, tacky stuff, and not a bit of style to any of it. What good-looking middle-aged woman/gal/babe wants to wear a pair of purple polyester pull-ons with a striped polyester long-sleeved shirt to match? And those shoes that they sell—hideous!

The models in these catalogs are young women, probably in their 30's, that are thinking to themselves, *I wouldn't be caught dead in this stuff!* Where are my tight jeans, boots, and cleavage-showing shirt? They probably pay them very well to model that sort of thing and want the ones that get the catalog to say, "Well they're wearing it, must be the new fashion!" *Barf!*

Getting back to my relative, I try to take her shopping, but she gets a little miffed with me when I tell her in a nice way that she dresses like an old lady. She pretends to ignore me, keeps looking in the wracks in the stores, and I keep pulling out things that would look good on her. Nope! She keeps heading for the polyester and the old drab colors. If she still smoked, she'd probably set herself on fire with all of that flammable material. *Shut my mouth!*

Now, on occasion, she will listen to me if I tell her that something really would look good on her. And it is usually something that I would wear and may have actually come out of my closet. She is not easy to convince and will usually find something wrong with it. Too short, not short enough, too long, not long enough, shows too much, doesn't fit right, doesn't fit at all, on and on. I don't know why I try so hard; just don't like to see anyone suffer over fashion sense. Heck, who am I kidding, I'm the one that is suffering, just watching the whole shebang!

When she comes to visit me, I usually have to change at least one thing on her so that we can go out in public. No dog slide with a fancy dress—change that! No high water jeans—throw those out, buy more. No black shoes and a brown pocketbook—change that or no pocketbook. No knee-high hose and flat shoes with jeans—take this off, buy boots and socks. Ditch the hose altogether. No baggy shirt if you want to look good. Quit trying to cover up all of your assets or your male friend/husband/significant other won't think you have any.

Whew! I'm exhausted from all of this fashion talk. I really do work hard to help this person look good when I get a chance. I think about my friend Nan that is older than this person, and she dresses more stylish than I do. And she doesn't care about her age. Heck, she is proud of the fact that she can still wear young, fashionable clothes well at this stage in her life. She doesn't try to cover up anything that matters, but I shouldn't be saying that. But I am one to speak my mind, so I'm saying it anyway.

So, I'll keep working with the other person in my life, and hope that one day she will listen. Come to think of it, some of my other relatives are and were very stubborn when it came to not dressing for their best. Remember my Aunt Linda? Couldn't light a firecracker under her and make her change her mind. Nope, wasn't going to happen on her time. I tried to get her to cut her hair once so that it would be short and stylish, and she argued me out of the room. I never tried again. She had long hair for almost all of her life; silvery gray and all!

I also tried to get her to go shopping with me a long time ago, and she very politely told me no! I can't remember her ever going shopping, at least not in my adult life. She had no use for a wardrobe and told you rightfully so. My Nanny was the same way and her mother before her. Just wasn't important to them. Now they might wear it if you gave it to them; maybe, maybe not! I would bet on the latter.

One time I gave my Nanny a nice new pair of bedroom shoes and a nice housecoat, as we call it. I was sick and tired of her wearing this old, raggedy, stained housecoat that she had and torn up shoes, but she was comfortable in them. Mind you, she could afford better, and carried a wad of money in her pocketbook that would *choke a horse*. But that's beside the point!

I gave her those clothes with a hint that she would throw the other ones away. Nope! She was saving them for a special occasion and put them in a drawer. And bless my *sweet britches*; she continued to wear the raggedy torn up ones until she could use them for a dust rag. And guess what I found when we cleaned out her house when she died? You guessed it!

Well, I suppose it is hard for people to change when they get older. LORD knows it's hard for me to change now! And I won't unless you can give me a dang good reason. So I guess I'll lay off of my relative about her fashion sense, 'cause I have run out of firecrackers. But just for the record, I don't want anyone ever to tell me that I dress like an old lady, even though I might be one someday. I would much rather be known as a sexy senior citizen, and they better lay it on thick!

Happy shopping, ya'll, and leave the polyester alone! But if you find that you have to retrain a relative or a friend, be nice! They just might tell you to go and mind your own dang business and quite minding theirs. So if they want to go ahead and wear the *"high-water"* britches, just let them go ahead, and pray for rain.

the BEAUTY SALON IS NOT A PLACE *for* SCREAMING YOUNG-UNS!

ood LORD in Heaven, do Southern women, or just women for that matter, love to go to a salon and get all *"doodied up,"* as my grandmother used to say. Yes we do and amen to that! I love to spend all day in one where I can expense it from my husband's bank account, but when it comes out of mine, probably just a wash, cut, and style. Might not work for him, but works for me!

The reason that I love going to get *doodied up* is because it is a place where I can be pampered, waited on hand and foot, and get to relax a bit before I have to go back to my real life or my real job or my real family. I just love to escape for a while, listen to soft music, listen to other people's business, look at other women or men with their hair plastered on their head, and just look and listen.

This is all good and something that I need about every six to eight weeks, and as far as I'm concerned, this is *my time*. I can handle the little white noises that I just mentioned, but I can't handle it when somebody brings a screaming child or several little not well-behaved young-uns to my shrine. It totally rear-ranges the mood and makes me want to become a raving maniac! And I ain't exaggeratin' either!

What are these mothers thinking when they bring these children or little *"put their hands on everything"* beings into a place like this? What are they thinking, and I am screaming this right now! Do they know that this is the only time every six to eight weeks that the rest of us have a moment's peace and would like to have our *moment?* Forgive me for being downright selfish right now, but I have already had the little beings that put their hands on everything, and I do not want to have to deal with round two!

Let me give you some examples of my pain at this time. I went into a nail salon once and this woman was sitting at a manicure table and was chatting away with the manicurist with her nails in small bowls. Beside her was a baby carrier with an infant in it. Well, this infant started to cry and started to arch his/her back in the infant carrier with his/her safety strap on. Mom kept right on chatting, and then reached over and gave the baby a sealed bottle of nail polish to bite on and play with. (Mind you, it came off the display for people to buy. And it had everybody else's germs on it, and it was nasty as far as I'm concerned, but don't get me started!)

Mom kept on chatting and getting her nails done, and the infant got tired of playing with the bottle of nail polish. I think I was the only one that was truly paying this infant any attention. The infant started *pitching a fit* and started to slide in the infant carrier and proceeded to slide out of the bottom of it still attached to the safety strap. Mom, by this time, had a fresh coat of polish on her nails, and there was no way in heck that she could have picked that infant up, much less unbuckled the safety strap so it wouldn't choke the baby.

Well, up I jumped, Mom's nail polish still intact, and picked up the infant and unbuckled the safety strap before we had a real casualty on our hands. Mom still had her nail polish intact and was still allowing the manicurist to continue. *What the heck again*, I thought!

I took the infant with me over to the sofa where I was sitting and bounced this baby on my knee until Mom finished and her nails had dried. So much for my relaxing wait and reading all the trash magazines that I could before it was my turn. Mom still didn't turn around but a time or two while I had the infant, never once said thank you or apologized for my interruption, just kept on finishing what she had come into the salon for. Obviously, it was not to take care of that infant!

If I had ever wanted to swat someone up side the head with my pocketbook, this was the time. I didn't blame the infant, just the mother over there that had no manners and no common sense! Leave the infant at home, lady, with a babysitter, or pay me for your services. That would just about pay for my manicure! *Shut my mouth!* No, no … not this time.

Then come to find out after she was done and out the door with that poor infant, that she was a local "whatever," chiropractor, veterinarian, but who cares! Certainly not me! She almost choked her infant because she didn't want to mess up her nails. I really should have swatted her with my pocketbook and taken the kid to Child Protective Services. *Whew…I'm fired up now!*

Another time I went to get my hair done, and this mother brought in three children with her and had them watch her get her hair done. Ha! Everybody was looking at the kids while they were there, and you can guess that they were not well-behaved little darlings. Should have put all of them on a hook on the wall! I would have tried if I could have found the hook. *Wanna give me a hammer!*

One was jumping up and down on the sofa, while I heard, *"Son, please stop! Sit down now! Be a good boy!"* You think a four-year-old is going to listen to that and behave when you are in restraints with a hairdresser? I think not! You'd have better luck trying to get your dog to do that! And I'm not kidding either. I think my dog Megan could do it!

The four-year-old continued to jump while the baby in the stroller started crying, and the other child, probably around five or six, totally ignored the other two. This older child wanted to put his hands on every bottle that was in the nail polish wrack. You remember what I said about little beings that put their hands on everything? This kid was no exception.

Their mom, , bless her heart, looked like she was *"fit to be tied."* At least she had some guilt over her children acting like little monsters, but she did bring them in here, so I couldn't feel too sorry for her. She really looked like she could use a rest, really needed a little glamour or "doodie-ing up," and definitely needed a babysitter so she could come in here in peace. *Could you blame her?*

But it still doesn't excuse the fact that someone

with misbehaving children brought them into my *shrine* (me and the other women) and disturbed my or our serenity. Don't they have any marbles in their head? Do they realize that we have only a few minutes or hours to get our sanity back and that they are intruding? And that while they are keeping us from getting our sanity back that we are probably going to be leaving half crazy? And do you think they care? *Probably freaking not!*

I do get worked up, don't I? Sorry... but heck fire and brimstone, stuff like this just irritates the crap out of me! I think that all of the salons should have a sign on the door with big and bold letters that says, *"This is not a circus or a side show, so leave the monkeys at home!"* But do I really think that these *"don't care"* mothers would take the hint! Probably not! And this is just to tick the rest of us that don't have little "put hands on everything" off.

So the next time I go to a salon and I am in the presence of an undisciplined mother with a few little darlings in tow, I think I'll just go up and swat her with my pocketbook before I have a chance to think about it or the kids have a chance to start misbehaving. Certainly would make me feel better. No... I'll just suppress that thought, 'cause it ain't ladylike, and it ain't Christian, and I should feel sorry for the poor undisciplined mother.

But who am I kidding! The pocketbook swatting would be the most revengeful thing that I have ever done again and again. The kids would probably be so shocked that they just might sit down and be quiet due to sheer fright and wait for an encore! Well... let me see if I can find my Aigner bag, the one with the chain link shoulder strap.

Here's to a quiet and peaceful salon experience, ya'll! Keep your pocketbook close, 'cause you know how to use it! Or maybe you can take up a collection for these unfortunate Moms and pay for them to buy gas to the next salon a few miles away. And include their service tip, and a stop at the nearest hardware store for a hook for each child. Works for me! And I'm going now!

I'M A NURSE BY TRADE
... *but* PLEASE DON'T
SHOW ME YOUR CRACK AT
A COCKTAIL PARTY!

ou think I'm kidding, don't you? Does anyone realize what kinds of crazy things happen to those of us that call ourselves a nurse? Do you have any idea how some people react when they find out that you are in the healthcare business? Well in case you didn't know, honey, you are fixing to get an ear full.

Sometimes when you tell people you are a nurse or whatever you are in the healthcare field, they seem to want to tell you their whole life story and all of their ailments whether you want to hear it or not! I have gotten cornered by a lot of people in my life that have told me everything from the fungus on their feet, to their current genital dysfunctions, the breast implants that they had and wish they hadn't, all the way to the heavy duty wax in their ears. I wished at that point that I had had a lot of wax in my ears so that I didn't have to listen to all of that!

I might be exaggerating a little bit, but I did have a man ask me to follow him in the bathroom after my revealing of being in the healthcare profession so he could show me the hemorrhoid that was protruding from his crack! I don't think so! No bathroom calls for me. Did I forget to mention that I was at a party with a cocktail dress on? I don't exactly bring gloves and KY jelly with me when I go to such occasions, just in case a *crack* emergency comes along. *Heaven forbid!*

I'm awful and I know it, but this kind of stuff needs to be said. People just sort of lose all dignity and their minds when they come face to face with a real live nurse that will actually stand there and listen to them. Lords knows, and I can also vouch for this, in the hospital or the doctor's office they hardly give you ten minutes at a time unless you have *messed* in your pants. I know that is an awful thing to say too, probably disgusting, but I think some folks might actually do it just to get some attention for ten more minutes. *Shut my mouth!*

No really, health care professionals, if they are actually working, don't have a lot of time to talk unless you are paying them by the hour! Then you are probably there for counseling or something like that, so they won't have time to look at your crack; that's extra. Here I go again, so I'll just stop with the crack insinuations.

When I was working as a floor nurse, or rather as a glorified, underpaid handmaiden to many, and I don't mean any disrespect by that, I had some of the dernd-est things happen to me. I've had men pinch my *girls*, try to pat my tush, try to pull me down, and want to show me things that I had no medical reason to see except to bathe with soap and water, to slap a bandage on it, or put a catheter in it. Ah! It can be quite hysterical, but some of my little old men, on medication or not, thought they were so slick and sexy, and some of their comments absolutely killed me with laughter! I never took them seriously, just got the heck out of the way and referred them to another unsuspecting professional. I usually let their doctor find out about it the hard way; but it's my secret.

Getting back to exposing yourself when you tell people you're a nurse, they really do try to tell you their life story! They seem to feel a connection to you and think it's okay to expose all of their inner secrets and their outer ones too! I don't think they realize that being a nurse is a job, something that all of us went to school to do, and not something that put a tattoo on our forehead that says *tell me all your dirty little secrets.*

Really, if people know it, they will come up to you in the grocery store, the public bathroom, at church, in the lunch line, at your child's school, call you on the phone at all hours, stop you while you're walking your dog, call you because they're a friend of so and so's, pull up beside you on the street, at the shopping mall, in a restaurant, and even talk to you under a bathroom stall! *It's the dang truth.* I'm not lying, because it has all happened to me.

How funny is that when you are in a bathroom stall and someone's hand waves at you from the other stall because they need a piece of toilet paper and then say, "Can you discuss my *problems* while we're both sitting here?" Not! That is the time that you take care of business, quickly flush, wash, and get the heck out of there! Suddenly you decide that you might want to change your name, change occupations, and where you live, and get another identity. *Enough of that!*

I have been in healthcare for over thirty years, (I'm showing my age, but I started when I was ten), and my experiences and near misses with people could fill several volumes, and this might just be the serious stuff. The hysterical stuff would double that! I have enjoyed most of my time serving the sick and injured public, even though a lot of it has and just might give me ulcers, high blood pressure, migraine headaches, muscles spasms and tics, and a psychiatric diagnosis. *You think I'm kidding don't you?*

A white uniform is a dead giveaway that you are in the healthcare profession, or you might just be in the food industry, or you are in the Navy. I wonder why they chose white since it starts getting dirty from the time that you put it on with all sorts of *"not so nice"* body fluids, which I won't name here! And you stare at them the whole time to see it slowly getting dirtier. Why couldn't they have chosen something that hides *stuff* a little better, like beige or brown or blue? Works for me!

Well, nursing and the healthcare profession really is rewarding work, no matter how strange the people are that you meet while you are doing it. Hospital nursing is funny stuff, especially in the emergency department. I guess that's why I stayed there for so many years; never a dull moment. And I think you have to be a special person to work in that area, maybe a little *warped,* and most of the people that know me would not beg to differ.

People from all walks of life come in there; the good, the bad, and the incredibly ugly; ugly-acting or ugly-looking! I've had them dressed to kill or dressed in rags or hardly dressed at all. I've seen them happy, sad, crying, yelling, swearing, fighting, laughing, psychotic, worried, neurotic, irritable, scared, and anxious, you name it. I've had to try to handle them in all situations, because that is what I was being paid to do, especially if you are the first nurse that they see when they come in the door—a little thing called the triage nurse. And guess what? You get to hear their whole life story first, and then maybe the reason that they came into the emergency department.

They tell you the darndest things too! And my question is, "You put a toothbrush holder where? Tell me again how many beers you've had? This is two-beer day, I'll just add you to the list. You've had that pain how many days, and you're just now coming in? How many pain pills did you take to make your speech slur that bad? You haven't had a bowel movement in how many days, and it's an emergency at four o'clock in the morning? You're coming in because your hair hurts? You stuck an M & M up your nose? Peanut or plain? You took turns shooting each other in the foot? You just have a stomachache? (Turned out she delivered a premature infant.) You came in here just to get something to eat? And the cake topper is, you drove yourself through the ED door in your car, because you had to *pee* really bad? And I could go on and on and on.

I love my job! I love my job! And I try to say that at least once a week whether I think it's true or not. I love writing too, because I get to tell all of the stuff that I have had to live through and how funny it is. Life is a story, and can be a funny one at that, so I guess I'll keep on writing.

So this is a thumbs up to all of us nurses and health-care professionals that have had to endure all of the craziness that our professions have had to offer us. But I consider us special people to do what we do, to the zany personalities that a lot of us have, and that we continue to do what we do and do it rather well.

So here's to us, ya'll! But tell your next stalker to keep their pants on!

P.S. I just went to the drugstore and heard a couple loudly discussing what type of wart remover to get. I had to control myself not to give them some advice because I am a nurse. Ah...just saved myself from another stalking story!

IT'S A DANG SHAME WHEN YOU HAVE TO TAKE YOUR LAPTOP TO *the* TOILET!

I don't watch too much television, but when I do, I believe what I see is real. At least part of the time! My *idea* of a writer creating their novel or whatever is in a place of calm, surrounded by beauty and serenity, high on a hilltop in a resort-like setting with nothing but peace and quiet. The lone typewriter or laptop on a large mahogany or oak antique roll top desk, expensive furnishings and fabrics, white linen curtains blowing in the breezes, the writer in a starched white shirt with pressed pants and a cup of coffee on a little pedestal, designer "readers" on their nose and a dog at their feet. What a picture!

And now I say horse hockey! And I say it loud and clear! I am only a rookie writer, but just from the little experience that I have had, at least in my household, there ain't no serene hilltop, peace and quiet, or curtains blowing in the breezes. There might be yelling and loud music, the dog barking at everything that passes, the television blaring, my family members talking on their cell phones so loud that I can't think at all, and someone is always asking me, "What's for supper?" That's my picture, and it ain't pretty!

So how do great writers find peace and quiet? They build themselves an office or buy themselves an estate in the country because they can afford it. For the rookies like me, that have a regular job, I have to find peace and quiet wherever I can, and it just might be the only place in my house that I can definitely be alone—the bathroom, the toilet, the loo, the outhouse, whatever you want to call it. *If I can't be alone in there, I can't be alone anywhere!*

I have also tried to find quiet by just going out to my car and sitting in it. It gets a little warm or a little cold depending on the time of year. And I don't want to keep the motor running to use the air conditioner 'cause I am afraid of gas fumes. Or I could just go to the library or the bookstore and take my laptop, but that defeats the purpose of trying to work at home. *Home* is not a serene place, so why try to kid myself?

Twice I have gone to the summer cottage of Ernest Hemingway, one of the greatest writers of all times. He had a separate area outside of the house that you had to go across a "catwalk" to get to from the main house. It was a nice cozy, quiet place that overlooked the swimming pool. He had a beautiful old oak table with his manual typewriter sitting there, and I thought, *Ah...all writers should have these places!* Not! At least not in my household.

Like I said, I am just a rookie, probably would call me a rookie at being a rookie since I haven't even published my first book yet, and hope I will be lucky enough to publish this one. I think my family gets aggravated with me sitting with my computer in my lap all the time and writing, but isn't that what I'm supposed to be doing? How in the heck do you think a book gets written? *By itself?* I do have another full-time job, you know, so I can only write when I am off or after work. It's okay though, 'cause by the time I get home and sit down, and writing is relaxing to me, in comes my dang family (and I mean it as a term of endearment) and interrupts every thought that I had!

"What's for supper? Where did you put the channel changer? That's all you do is sit and type on that laptop. Did you go by the grocery store today? What's for supper? (Again.) Have you taken the dog out? I don't feel good!"

Ya da, ya da, ya da! I just want to yell at the top of my lungs, please just kiss my assets, and let me work! But if I did they would just laugh at me, look like deer in the headlights, and get mad at me because I don't jump to their every request. I think I'll go to Mr. Hemingway's house and ask them if I can use his quiet room. But knowing my dang family, they'd find me there!

My primary job is working forty hours as a registered nurse in one of the local hospitals. I stay there all day, and then come home and try to write until bedtime. Then every day, except weekends and holidays, I repeat the process. Writing is therapy for me, and I enjoy it immensely. It gives me a chance to relive and even recreate my past. But just when the ideas, the sentiment, and the sassiness start to flow, someone in my not-so-quiet household will come and ask me something, and then I lose all train of thought. *Dang it!*

There is definitely such a thing as *"writer's block,"* and I go through it several times a week. I write a while, then I'll have to put it down when the thoughts slowly stop coming, then I'll have to regenerate, and then come back to it at a later time. Maybe wait even a day or two. If I wait a while, the ideas will start flowing again, and I'll go right back to where I started. I guess that's just part of the process, and everybody probably goes through it. I suppose that is why it takes months and even years to write a book. *And I can see why*! And when you have three people at home that don't know how to fix their own supper, it takes even longer.

I'm getting tickled or ticked off at my family right now. My daughter Kelli came in, talking on her cell phone, and was trying to decide if she wanted to go out with the guy that two hours ago she was never going to go out with again. Then she sat down on the couch while I was trying to type and started staring at me silently. *Can't stand that*! I would rather she just talk away and totally interrupt my train of thought. After I keep typing for a few minutes, she finally gets up and says she's going to check her email on the other computer. Yes…please…go now…can I show you the way…? Now let me get back to my book, for heaven's sake!

Then…my son Josh comes in with his laptop and sits right smack dab next to me on the sofa. Not two inches are between us and he starts typing loudly! Can't do it softly…lo*udly*! Then he starts talking to himself, hitting his heels on the footstool, cracking and popping his knuckles, and totally blocking my train of thought again. *I'm going to smack him!* Love him to death, but I am just about ready to get in the smack mode.

My channel-flipping husband has got the television on so loud that I have had to tell him to turn it down about three times. The neighbors are going to tell him to turn the channel next, since he has it up so loud. *Hearing problem, my behind!* He just uses it as an excuse to tick me off. I can recite everything the television is saying, and I don't give a rat's behind that the men on TV got lucky and have a pair of sixes, and that one of them has diamonds or whatever. *Dang poker!* I just want him to turn it down or off so I can think! But... there ain't no chance in that happening tonight. Then he flips the channel to wrestling, then to poker again, and I have just about had it. I am just about ready for smack down too or just give me a pair of aces, and call it a night!

No wonder writers take so long to write a book, and if they have a family it's a wonder if it gets written at all. I guess I feel a little better though, since I think that most writers, unless they have a separate house or leave town, probably have a family around to help annoy them while they are trying to write too. And I can just see it now: my favorite Miss Dottie writing another New York Times bestseller and her family coming to her and asking "What's for supper?" or "Where did you put the channel changer?" And I can also just bet she has a New York Times bestselling answer to give them too!

So if you're brave enough, happy writing, ya'll! And if you're smart enough, *leave town!*

KIDS REALLY SHOULD COME WITH AN INSTRUCTION MANUAL!

I heard this on the radio the other day, just a little differently, so I have to elaborate on it a bit. Just might step on some toes here, so if you're one of *"those"* parents, please excuse me and go see a child psychologist. 'Cause this little bit of information is for you, honey child!

I was doing what I do best on a Sunday afternoon, shopping in the mall with *no* money! Not really, I was just strolling through the back of one of the stores by the shoe department and heard very loudly the derndest thing come out of a woman's mouth: "Are YOU going to get a pair of tennis shoes now or aren't you?" It wasn't the phrase so much, as her tone of voice!

I couldn't help but look in that direction, and I was expecting a teenager or maybe an older child, but this little boy was about five years old! He just sat there and hung his head, not sassing or anything. He was just sitting there, and his mother, I guess that was who she was, was talking loud enough for the whole store to hear her! Or rather the whole mall could hear her.

I walked around to the display across from the shoe department and heard her continue to rant and rave at this poor child. If I have ever wanted to smack someone up side the head with my pocketbook or any other heavy thing that I could pick up, this was the time! I felt my stomach getting into knots, my blood pressure going up, and I just wanted to let that woman have a piece of my mind. And it wouldn't have been "How ya doin'?" but a big *smack!*

I just wonder what in the heck she was thinking? I should have said, "Ma'am, he is just about five years old, and you want him to make a decision if he gets a pair of tennis shoes or not? Do you also want him to settle the national debt, pick the next president, and decide when we're gonna go to the moon next? (I could volunteer to smack her there!) Do you not have the God-given brains to make that decision for him? I guess not, considering the racket you are making. Is the ceiling going to cave in if he doesn't give you an answer now? I don't think so, and if it does cave in, I hope it falls totally on you!" *Shut my mouth!*

I hate to see a momma or a daddy totally try to humiliate their children. You know, in case you haven't figured it out, kids don't come with an instruction manual, so I hope to the good LORD that he gives them to the right people. But as you and I both know, that is not the case a lot of the time. And the way that woman was talking to that little boy, I doubt if she did have an instruction manual that she would have taken the time to read it. Heck, she couldn't even make a decision as to whether the little boy needed to get a new pair of tennis shoes or not! Dumb broad! *Shut my mouth again!*

I think children are a blessing, and they do not deserve not to be hollered at for no reason. Maybe if they deserved it, but gently puh…lease, and not for tennis shoes indifference. *Just get the dang shoes, lady!*

If a child misbehaves, like sassing their momma or daddy, kicking the dog, fighting with their sibling, sticking their tongue out (*I totally detest that one!*), or cussing where your parents could hear you, that probably deserves some attention. But maybe hollering might not be the proper punishment, but sitting in the corner would be perfect.

Do you remember sitting in the corner, and how you hated it? I had to stick my nose in the corner of the wall and couldn't look around or nothing. If I got caught, my momma would add five more minutes to my punishment, and there ain't nothing worse than being a hyperactive kid and being made to be still. Pure torture as far as I was concerned! And that corner standing seemed like it went on for hours, and I hated that punishment with a passion.

If there was such a thing as a kids' instruction manual, I think "New and Creative Ways to Torture your Child" would be on the front page. And I think corner standing would be the number one torture. Number two torture would probably be washing your mouth out with soap if you said a *bad* word or cussed.

I think I did have my mouth washed out a few times, and it was probably with Ivory soap. Ew! I can still feel Momma's hands in my mouth while she was doing that, and I think I did try that on my own kids a time or two. Didn't keep them or me from misbehaving though! I think we just weighed the odds that we would get caught, knew what would happen if we did, and then went ahead and did it just for the thrill of it.

You know kids aren't dumb, and we should give them way more credit than we do!

Another chapter in the kids' instruction manual might be what to do when they have a temper tantrum. How many times did your little darling suddenly arch their back, get on the floor and start kicking and screaming at the top of their lungs? Refuse to walk or just sit on the floor and refuse to get up? Hmm…not very many in my household. I just walked over them and let them scream their head off, turned the television up a little louder if we were in the house, and ignored everything the child was doing. Pretty soon my little darling would usually come to me with a poked out lip, a runny nose, and a glare in their eyes. After I still refused to give in to this type of behavior, they might sit beside me or down by my feet. Then after another few minutes, and *frigid* attention by their momma or daddy, they might try to sit in one of our laps. Then they might get some attention. Just about worked every time! If this didn't, they usually got a swat on the butt! Then that worked very nicely thank you!

I wasn't one for corporal punishment with my kids, or as they call it nowadays, child abuse! Yes, my children did get a minor paddling a time or two or three or four, maybe more than that, but they knew I meant business. Phrases like "sweet little darlings, now sit down and be good for Momma" sounds like a bunch of hogwash to a kid. Especially to mine! I raised two little hellions (it's now a term of endearment), or rather they raised me, and if I would have said that to them, they would have laughed me out of the house. But if I said, " Now, you two little kids, sit your dang butts down now or I'm gonna beat yours!"

(I was probably a little more colorful, but that ain't nice, so I'll just leave it at that.) *Silence!* If not, I would just put the punishment toward my channel-flipping husband, say good night, get a glass of wine, and go to bed. Husbands are good for something. *Amen!*

Getting back to that instruction manual for kids; God knew what he was doing by not providing one. Hopefully he gives most kids smart parents so that they figure out how to deal with them. Parenting is a hard job, and it takes a lot of effort, patience, and a lot of creativity to try to do a half decent job and a whole lot of hollering to do a very good job! Hollering, not really, but it does come in very handy a lot of the time. I have decided that when my kids were growing up, I was an expert at it, but as I've gotten older, I've lost my hollering touch and have toned it down to *normal* speech again.

But mind you, they are now grown young adults, and I am retired from that behavior. Plus, I am now on an excellent set of drugs that make me very happy! (*They are legal, so keep your pants on!*) Where were these when my kids were growing up and I really needed them? At that point in my life I thought that hollering and almost having a nervous breakdown was *normal* when you were raising kids without a manual. I didn't realize at the time that maybe I needed a crutch like "happy pills," but my good ole doctor at the time never suggested such a thing. (He was also a man, so that tells you a lot! He probably didn't stay at home the majority of the time with his kids either!)

When you come from a generation of hollerers like I have, this behavior probably seems normal. Me, my momma, Nanny, Aunt Linda, my great grandmother, and I probably could go on and on if I thought about it for a little while; must be the Scotch-Irish temper. *Yeah, that's it!* We are and were all great hollerers, but guess what? We got our point across and did raise some not too bad kids without a manual.

So, does childrearing really require a manual? I don't think so. Nobody has ever had one, except for Dr. Spock. And I think that book went out with the dark ages and doesn't go much past babyhood. The rest of the kid's life is the really fun part! And a very good learning experience for every parent. So when their kids are grown, they can sit back and watch their own kids with their children and smile with delight when they hear their kids hollering at their grandchildren. *Ah…the memories and the* sweet revenge!

But when it comes down to buying tennis shoes, just be a good momma and do it! Or if you hear some lady yelling *"ouch"* in the shoe department and *"that pocketbook came out of nowhere!"* I didn't do it!

Case closed, ya'll!

A FACE LIFT, LIPOSUCTION, *and* BOTOX ... HAPPY BIRTHDAY TO ME!

I just have to write a little bit here about the many wonders of the plastics industry. Every newspaper, magazine, and some television ads that I see or read have advertisements and enticements related to some type of erasure of every body flaw that you could possibly have! Heck, I probably could get a whole new one if I played my cards right! Just go on the internet, check the appropriate boxes, send in the appropriate fee, click on submit, and *voila!* Your new body will be on its way in 5–7 business days via general delivery or overnight express if you prefer for an extra $14.95. Wouldn't it be great if it were that simple? *Or that insane!*

I don't know! Maybe that is too simple. Is there really anything so terribly wrong about just aging gracefully and welcoming the little lines, wrinkles, bulges, and varicose veins that come with getting older and wiser? *Heck fire and yes there is!* When I grow old gracefully without kicking and screaming, that will be the day that Hell freezes over!

I just had my *big* birthday last year, and I *d-double-*

dared my husband to have a big party to welcome the other half century part of my life! I told him absolutely not, don't even think about it, and I better not have any surprises. No black balloons, no sick cards, no bad jokes, and he better not get me anything with a hat on it! I think that kind of stuff is perfectly fine for other ladies, just not for me! I am definitely not an old lady, and if you say I am, you can just *kiss my assets!* Whew...I'm fired up and need to *shut my mouth!* I warned you I was outspoken and tell the truth absolutely.

I'm sorry to sound so harsh, but that stuff is just not for me! I used to think it was funny to pull that kind of humor on other people, but when it came around to being my turn, I said "no thank you," and I'll break your arm or your face if you do! It's not a big joke to me to be getting another decade older or welcoming less than the second half of my life. *Not funny at all!* If someone had had a party for me, I don't think I would have laughed at all, but probably would have cried and embarrassed the heck out of myself. Ain't a dang thing funny about getting older! It just means you're going out sooner!

Well, I did intend to celebrate my birthday, but I wanted to celebrate it *my* way. Quietly...and would welcome any gifts like a certificate to a spa for a massage, facial, manicure, pedicure, or a salt scrub. Now that's what I call a personal party; just me, myself and I, for the entire day. No tacky crap from the party shop to make me want to cram it into the person that gave it to me. I do tend to get a little volatile when someone tries to kid me about being old!

I did get my spa day on my birthday, and I enjoyed

every blessed minute of it! Cleansed, scrubbed, exfoliated, moisturized, massaged, painted, and finished off with a bottle of mineral water and a bowl of strawberries while I was wrapped in an ultra soft robe and matching slippers, in a lounge chair with pillows to my back, soft music with a trickling water fountain, low diffuse lighting, and no black balloons anywhere! *Awesome!*

Now my birthday did not end here. While I was being pampered to perfection, I was browsing through one of those "I don't subscribe because they are too expensive magazines" and saw an advertisement for another day spa that did facial treatments: dermabrasion, Botox, mineral makeup, etc. And it was just a short drive from my house. *Bingo!*

Since I was in the mood to improve myself, I decided that I would just make an appointment and see what this was all about. Since I had already taken off the first layer of my natural skin with all of this pampering etc., maybe it wouldn't take too much effort to start working towards getting the *new* face that I *thought* I wanted. I just didn't know at the time that it was a lot more involved than I realized.

So I decided to call the mystery spa and give it a shot. I didn't have a dern thing to lose except maybe a few wrinkles, lines, some of my age spots, and my husband's money. Heck, maybe if they could do that good of a job, maybe my age would look more like the previous decade instead of this one. Fat chance, but it was worth a shot!

Got me an appointment, drove down to the place, walked inside and sat down. *Prim and proper little thang, ain't it*, I thought. It was definitely aesthetic-looking;

magazines and pictures all over the place with before and after photos, makeup samples, moisturizers, wrinkle reducers, collagen enhancers, line smoothers, lip plumpers, sun screens, anything you wanted. If they had just had a handsome man wrapped in cellophane for takeout, it would have been perfect. *Shut my mouth!*

My name was called, and I walked into a small room with a lot of sterile-looking things in it. Mind you, I am a nurse, but some of those things looked a little scary to be *messing* with my face. It looked more like a dentist office or an operating room. Wasn't too sure if this is what I had in mind. I preferred the pampering session that I had on my birthday, and thought that maybe this would be an extension of that. I didn't see a trickling fountain anywhere or an ultra soft robe! *Hmm.!*

A pretty, sterile-looking young lady walked in that matched the room and talked to me for about an hour. She was about thirty-five or maybe younger, and she told me that she had already had dermabrasion, Botox, and was thinking about some other procedures. I looked at her and thought, *what the heck? I'm about fifteen years older than she is, and she is already way ahead of me!* She talked to me some more and told me about some of the side effects to expect, and I guess I didn't have a clue that there would be any! At least not in my present mind!

She then told me that your face might turn red and then peel, it wouldn't move like it used to, some of the muscles above your brow would be paralyzed, and on and on! The more she said, the less I was amused, and the more I was liking how my face looked normally. If I was going to have my face peel off and not move the *normal* way, then I might as well go down to the beach, drink a bottle of wine, get a sunburn, let my skin peel naturally, and call it a day. Probably would do the same thing, only I wouldn't remember a whole lot about it! *Shut my mouth!*

So I left the pretty little day spa with the advanced procedures and decided that I would go home and watch the channel that was showing liposuction and a facelift procedure. Maybe this would be more up my alley, and you would be put under anesthesia to boot! Not sitting in some doctor's office wide-awake while he came towards you with his stainless steel instruments and needles. And not scaring the crap out of this Southern belle, 'cause I don't do needles well, or cold, hard instruments.

The show that I flipped to showed the facelift procedure first. *I was never so grossed out in all of my life!* The doctor looked like he was literally ripping a woman's face right off of her skull. He just kept shoving this instrument down into her face under her skin and the more he did this the more her face came off. He would then pull and snip! Ahhhhhhh! *There ain't no way in heck that I would do that!* I will just live with every blasted line and wrinkle that I have. Until they can find something that will work on the outside of my face and not have to pull it in all different directions and throw part of it in a stainless steel basin, *I will just deal with it!* Maybe get me a tight headband or something! Or move to a country where they have to wear head coverings. *Not!*

The next part of this saga showed a different *witch doctor* doing a liposuction procedure, and this made me absolutely want to lose my cookies, and I'm a nurse for Pete's sake! He was literally taking a hosepipe and shoving it under some poor soul's skin and applying suction to it like a vacuum cleaner. I can't make that sound on paper, but the suction sounded like when you use a can of whipped cream and you could see the fat running through the hosepipe! He just kept jabbing in all directions on the person's stomach, and I finally had to turn it off because I couldn't stand to watch the slaughter any longer!

Why in the name of insaneness would anyone want to do that? A facelift or liposuction on purpose? If I want to have myself purposely mutilated, just call Freddie Kruger, and I bet he would do it for free, and in one tenth of the time!

For all of this education that I have received, and the visuals that even I don't want to ever look at again, I have decided that I might as well age gracefully and let the lines and wrinkles begin. They really aren't so bad! Just put a ton of expensive makeup on them and you hardly even notice, especially if you have to use a spatula to put it on with. Or if worse comes to worse, just wear a scarf over your face and explain that it is your custom. You might even start a fad. Would be a whole lot less expensive than all of the other crap or having your face and body carved up like a pumpkin!

You know I'm kidding about all this, don't you? I don't want to age any more than the next vain woman, but its fun to talk about, isn't it? The things we women do to try to stay young and beautiful. And what I do enjoy is continuing to dip in my channel-flipping husband's bank account to pay for it all. Because…he did marry me so he could have the trophy wife…and a trophy has to be polished quite often…and it is my birthday...at least once a year...but to me it's my birthday all the time!

So enjoy, ya'll, and don't let anyone buy you one of those colored hats, no matter what age you are! Not unless they come with a strap that will make it stay on your head while you ride your motorcycle. And you have colored boots to match! And a coordinating scarf would be nice! Now that's more like it!

Have a sassy birthday, ya'll!

SOME SASSY SENTIMENTS
to LIVE BY ...

1) Laugh often and any time you feel like it!

Don't let other people determine when you're going to laugh. Laugh when you feel like it! And do it often. Life is too serious, so I engage in this activity all the time. It's contagious, you know. And if it disturbs somebody else, tell them to shut the door or *git gone!*

2) Dance, Dance, Dance!

Turn up the music and dance to the groove! We do this at work during our break and feel like we've really had a break. Don't just settle for a boring cup of coffee. Your dance partner can be a broom or the nearest IV pole or your boss if he happens to walk by! I've seen my boss dance, so I'll be looking him up!

3) Wear polka dots with your black dress!

Black is nice, but it can be boring. Jazz it up with polka dots or a vibrant bright color. It shows you are an individualist and don't mind being a little *snazzy*. It also shouts, "I am me and I love who I am," and you don't need anybody else to tell you that.

4) Love your family and friends!

We're all in this life together, and we might as well make the very best of it! Don't be afraid to give a hug, compliment, or show someone you care about them, even your weird relatives. It actually burns calories because it does take a little effort. And if you don't want to do this, be adopted by another *normal* family or find some *normal* friends. But a little abnormal is more fun!

5) Adopt a pet that doesn't have a home!

Give the gift of love to an unwanted animal. This can be one of your greatest blessings. You give them love and get ten fold in return. Plus it can chase the neighbor's kids when you are tired of them playing in your yard. Ha! Or the unwanted, uninvited relatives when they show up on your doorstep.

6) When life gives you lemons, make a dang racket!

When things aren't going your way or you are just having a bad day, sit back, relax, and blow some *dragon breath*. You'll feel a lot better, and the noise that you make will make people leave you alone so you can recuperate. So after this is over, you can ask your husband for his credit card and go shopping, amen!

7) Eat dessert first and last!

What a way to greet and end a meal. Chocolate first and chocolate to finish it off! *Sounds good to me!* And besides, do you need anyone else's permission? I think not! Plus, if you want a little more padding on your tush, it's probably worth it. And not one man that I know has ever complained about any *little extra* there!

8) Never let anyone tell you, you can't!

And I mean this one. Do what you like and do it the best you can and do it well. Your life is your own, not anyone else's. And don't let anyone else tell you what to do. Or you can tell them to go and mind their own business, 'cause two people in yours is a little bit crowded. Do you think Scarlett did?

9) Befriend an older person!

They probably have more to tell you than you have to tell them. Many of them had been there, done that, and don't let those wrinkles fool you. Those are just mileage lines. I bet they know a thing or two that you don't. Listen and learn! And if you get tired of listening, turn off *your* hearing aide!

10) Be a friend to your older kids!

When they're growing up, you have to be more of a parent and not their buddy! When they are adults you can be their parent and their buddy too! It's a different relationship when they're older. But trading underwear secrets with your daughter is a little weird though! But we won't go there!

11) Middle age is the age for sports cars!

Go ahead, buy that car that you've always wanted. 'Cause, honey, you ain't getting any younger. Besides, it's only money, and you earn more of it every day. Might have to eat peanut butter more and buy less, but heck you got your car. And if your kids are grown, you only have to pay one gas bill. Unless your kids move back home like mine did! *Shut my mouth!*

12) If you don't like cat litter on your socks, get a dog!

Nothing to say here! If you complain about the mess then change animals. Or turn it around and say they need to change owners. But don't blame the cat! Who picked whom?

13) If you are Southern, embrace your heritage!

Don't hide from it or try to change your accent. Consider yourself special 'cause you were born and raised in a wonderful place. If you were born in the North, the Midwest, the East Coast, or Timbuktu, embrace your heritage too! Everyone has a special place.

14) If you get caught in the armpit of life, shave it!

I know this is corny, but true! If you get stuck in a rut in life, and don't feel like you can get out of it, just take it one day at a time!

Shave off some of the rut everyday, and pretty soon you might be back to normal. But if your normal is like mine, then it ain't!

15) *Its okay to shut up, but let your mind keep talking!*

I do a lot of thinking and really don't have to talk to a soul! But if someone does tell me to shut up, I am probably contemplating their demise in my head, and I am telling them a thing or two. If a woman talks, you know what she's thinking, if she doesn't—look out!

16) *Pretty is as pretty does, but what if you're downright ugly?*

Beauty is in the eye of the beholder, and how often have you heard that? That's just an excuse though for that guy that has no teeth and no fashion sense and keeps a bag of Big Red in his back pocket. But bless his heart he tries though and carries a silver-plated spit cup around with him so he doesn't get it on the floor or have it fly your way! And if his spit cup is silver plated, at least he has a little class; it could have been a Styrofoam cup.

17) *Don't ever take yourself too seriously!*

That says it! Humor is a gift, so enjoy it every day. You might get funny looks from people, and they might think you are strange, but you're the one having fun, and they're not! So who cares what they think anyway? Life's too short for pessimism!

Enjoy the sunshine! 'Cause rain will definitely ruin your makeup. But that's another book.

And I'm working on it, girlfriend!

AFTERWORD

I'm glad you could take part in a little bit of my Southern madness! You see, I love to laugh, laughter is a good thing, and I never take myself too seriously! I guess you could tell this by some of the stories that I have just told you.

So if you are Southern or a Southern transplant, I hope I did give you a little bit of *home* to take away with you. Home is an endearing word to me, and hopefully to most people, because it's where we all come from and the place that brings us the most joy, or creates the most insanity! *Shut my mouth!*

I like to tell stories about my family, have quite a few colorful characters in my family tree, and just gave you a taste of a few of them here. I couldn't tell about all of them, but if this book is enjoyed by many, I hope to write another one.

A lot of my inspiration, as I mentioned, came from the Southern coastal towns of Myrtle Beach and Murrells Inlet, South Carolina. Two of the most beautiful places in the South! This entire area is an inspiration to any artist or writer, and I consider myself a rookie at best.

So bless your heart and don't let anybody tell you to

shut your mouth! 'Cause we Southern gals have a lot to say, and we'll keep on talking till the cows come home!

Thank you again for letting me share my book with you. I plan to keep on writing every chance I get and also trying to get my family to learn to fix their own supper, plus a few other choice thangs. And that will be a lifelong chore for me! And as all good Southerners say, "Good to see, ya. Ya'll, come back now!"

Laugh a lot and always,

Kathy

FAMILY RECIPES

These are some of my *good ole family recipes* that were copied off of my grandmother's kitchen files and from my memory. They are among my most favorite, so I hope you enjoy every blessed one of them. And they are truly blessed, 'cause Southerners put a lot of heart and soul into what they cook. Enjoy!

Nanny's Plain or Blackberry Dumplings

These are some of the best things that you have ever put in your mouth, and this is the only recipe that you will probably ever find.

Plain Dumplings

2 C. plain flour

Pinch salt

1 egg

1T. Shortening

Water

2 C. of chicken broth (only for this version)

Sift the flour, add salt, and use a fork to blend the shortening into the flour. Beat the egg with ½ cup of water. Using fork, continue to blend the egg mixture in flour. Add small amounts of water until the dough leaves the sides of the bowl. Then roll the dough out thin around an 1/8 inch, then let it sit to dry. Cut into pieces to drop into boiling chicken broth.

Add the dumplings one at a time to keep from sticking, and cook until they are done!

Blackberry Dumplings

2 C. of fresh blackberries or canned if in a pinch.

1 C. sugar

Water to cover berries

Bring this berry mixture to a boil, and add the dumplings as prepared above, except leave out the chicken broth and use *water* instead to cook the dumplings in.

Once the dumplings are done, you may need to add sugar to taste.

Ain't nothing better!

Southern Sweet Tea

This is how my family has made it for generations!

To make a gallon of sweet tea:

4 regular size teabags

1–2 C. of sugar to taste

Water

Small teapot or any saucepan will do

Get ice-cold water, put in teapot, and add your teabags.

Place it on your stove and bring it to a boil.

Let it boil for a few minutes, then take it off the stove and let it steep. You can let it steep for as long as you like, the longer the better.

Pour the steeped mixture in a gallon jug or pitcher.

Add 1–2 cups of sugar, depending on how sweet you like your tea.

Stir until the sugar is dissolved.

Add water to fill the rest of the gallon container.

Stir again.

Put it in the refrigerator and let it get cold, if you can.

Or you can serve it immediately with crushed or cubed ice in a tall clear glass.

Add lemon slices or juice for a *twang,* or mint leaves for a nice touch.

Enjoy!

Homemade Southern Biscuits

This is how I used to make them, but it was from watching my momma and my Nanny the whole time I was growing up! And this recipe is purely from memory.

Self-rising flour

Crisco Shortening or Lard (Lard actually has the best flavor!)

Buttermilk

Preheat your oven to 465 degrees Fahrenheit

Find the deepest bowl you have, and sift about 2 cups of flour in it to make a "hill." On this hill, put about ½ cup of shortening or lard on it, so that it sinks into the hill making a well, and start pouring little bits of buttermilk into this. Grease up your hands with some of the Crisco or lard, and start mixing the flour, Crisco or lard and buttermilk in the well.

Use your hands, since biscuits turn out better this way. A fork or spoon just won't do as well. Mix the three ingredients together, slowly, but surely. Keep adding a little more buttermilk, taking in a little more flour, and vice versa. Mix from the middle and when your dough gets dry, add more milk, then more flour, etc.

When you get all of this mixed together, start folding it in and over on itself to create a ball of dough. Take a little bit more flour and sprinkle it on this ball so that it loses its outside stickiness. Don't handle it too much, 'cause your biscuits won't rise as well.

Sprinkle some more flour on your counter surface or pastry sheet and put your dough ball on it. Turn it over and over lightly until all sides of the ball are coated with flour. Now you are ready to roll it out to cut your biscuits or you can pinch your biscuits off in little balls.

For rolling:

Dust your pin with flour, roll your dough out, and cut with biscuit cutter or a glass will work. Put them on a cookie sheet or pan. You can separate them by 2 inches for individual crusty biscuits or bunch them together and pull them apart when done.

If you pull them apart, the sides will be soft.

For pinching:

Pinch off 2–3 inches round balls, roll them in your hands, then place them the same and pat slightly.

Cook in a hot oven for 12–15 minutes and until nicely brown. Serve immediately with butter or margarine, jams/jellies/preserves or nothing at all.

Homemade biscuits are absolutely delicious, but to make them the best, don't be concerned about using lard or Crisco. This is what makes them good; so don't go "light" on the ingredients. Besides, you don't eat them that often, and you want to do it up right!

Absolutely delicious!

Gran's Banana Pudding

No instant here! This is my momma's recipe and the kind that was there when I was a kid! People don't go to this much trouble anymore.

¾ C. of sugar

3 eggs, separated (yolk from white)

2 ½ T. of flour

Dash of salt

2 ½ C. whole milk

1 t. Vanilla

Vanilla wafers/cookies

4 whole bananas

¼ t. cream of tartar

½ C. of sugar

Preheat oven to 350 degrees Fahrenheit.

Mix together sugar, egg yolks, flour, and salt. Add milk and mix again. Heat over medium heat until thickened. Then add vanilla. You could probably use a double boiler for this, and make sure you stir constantly. This is your pudding mixture.

Layer vanilla wafers, then a layer of sliced bananas, and keep going to the top of the bowl. A round glass bowl that is oven safe is nice, if you have one. Pour the pudding mixture on top of this, so that it drizzles through the cookies and bananas.

For meringue:

Beat egg whites with ½ cup of sugar and cream of tartar, until you have a stiff peak. Put this on top of your pudding, cookie, and banana mixture. Put in 350-degree oven, for 15–20 minutes, this will set your meringue and brown it a little.

This is one beautiful pudding, and a fine accent to any table. Beats the heck out of the "quickie" kind. Make this, and it will be hard to go back to the fast batch. And don't skimp on the ingredients, and try to save calories; it's so worth it to eat a few more.

Let it cool before serving and enjoy!

e|LIVE

---

listen|imagine|view|experience

AUDIO BOOK DOWNLOAD INCLUDED WITH THIS BOOK!

In your hands you hold a complete digital entertainment package. Besides purchasing the paper version of this book, this book includes a free download of the audio version of this book. Simply use the code listed below when visiting our website. Once downloaded to your computer, you can listen to the book through your computer's speakers, burn it to an audio CD or save the file to your portable music device (such as Apple's popular iPod) and listen on the go!

How to get your free audio book digital download:

1. Visit www.tatepublishing.com and click on the e|LIVE logo on the home page.
2. Enter the following coupon code:
   9c07-e277-a855-bbbd-0259-26ae-d042-4dff
3. Download the audio book from your e|LIVE digital locker and begin enjoying your new digital entertainment package today!